# A Beginner's Guide to
# Acrylic Painting

## Tools, Surfaces, Mediums, & More...

Everything you need to know!

Written & illustrated by
Tonya Henderson

---

**Special <u>FREE</u> Bonus Gift for You**

To help you to achieve more success faster,
there are **FREE BONUS RESOURCES** for you at:

## Creative Spirit Studios

- "Five Essential Resources I Use in My Art Business"
- "The Ultimate Guide to Starting a Fine Art Painting Business"

First Edition Printing 1-15-2018

Second Edition Printing 6-11-2024

Copyright © 2018, 2023, 2024, 2025 Tonya Henderson

All rights reserved. No part of this publication may be reproduced, stored in a retrieval system, or transmitted in any form or by any means, electronic, mechanical, photocopy, recording, or otherwise, other than for "fair use" as brief quotations embodied in articles or reviews without prior written permission of the publisher. Doing so violates copyright law. Published by Tonya Henderson **Copyright © 2025 Tonya Henderson, Creative Spirit Studios LLC. ALL RIGHTS RESERVED.** No part of this book or its associated ancillary materials may be reproduced or transmitted in any form or by any means, electronic or mechanical, including photocopying, recording, or by any informational storage or retrieval system without permission from the publisher. **PUBLISHED BY:** Creative Spirit Studios. DISCLAIMER AND/OR LEGAL NOTICES While all attempts have been made to verify the information provided in this book and its ancillary materials, neither the author nor publisher assumes any responsibility for errors, inaccuracies, or omissions and is not responsible for any financial loss by the customer in any manner. Any slights of people or organizations are unintentional. EARNINGS & INCOME DISCLAIMER concerning the reliability, accuracy, timeliness, usefulness, adequacy, completeness, and/ or suitability of the information provided in this book, Tonya Henderson, Creative Spirit Studios LLC., its partners, associates, affiliates, consultants, and/or presenters make no warranties, guarantees, representations, or claims of any kind. Readers' results will vary depending on several factors. This book and all products and services are for educational and informational purposes only. Any examples, stories, references, or case studies are for illustrative purposes only and should not be interpreted as testimonies and/or examples of what readers and/or consumers can generally expect from the information. Any statements, strategies, concepts, techniques, exercises, and ideas in the information, materials, and/or seminar training offered are simply opinions or experiences and thus should not be misinterpreted as promises, typical results, or guarantees (expressed or implied). The author and publisher (Tonya Henderson and/or Creative Spirit Studios LLC. or any representatives) shall in no way, under any circumstances, be held liable to any party (or third party) for any direct, indirect, punitive, special, incidental, or other consequential damages arising directly or indirectly from any use of books, materials and or seminar training, which is provided "as is," and without warranties.

# WHAT OTHERS ARE SAYING ABOUT TONYA HENDERSON'S COURSES, MENTORSHIP, & ART

"For many years I struggled with keeping my focus on being a full-time artist. Often, I just found myself being derailed for one reason or another. My passion was calling, I wanted to make my living through the arts. It was time to get focused on me. Tonya helped me drill down my dreams with a vision of what I could do differently, a workable plan was born. As a caring and intuitive guide, she has quite a way of keeping you accountable to yourself."

—**Patt B.** *Student-Art Marketing Mentorship*


"You are just wonderful! I was drawn to you as God knew what I needed to hear, and you were the vessel! Thank you so much."

—**Joyce** *Coaching/Art Collector*


"I've had the pleasure of working with Tonya the artist and the entrepreneur, and both experiences were fantastic. She takes a compassionate, thoughtful approach to all her work and is able to help her clients understand what drives them and what hinders them better than anyone I've ever seen, which allows for genuine transformation to take place. If you get the opportunity to work with her, by all means, do it!"

—**Amanda B.** *Art Collector/Business Associate*


"Love the paintings. The two bird paintings add a touch of color and whimsy. Tonya was a delight. Responded to emails very promptly. Items arrived promptly and well packaged and even contained a sweet note from the artist."

—**Gretchen** *Art Collector*

"Tonya is an amazing mentor. She meets you where you are. She is committed to your success and offers her wisdom to get you where you want to go."

—**Chevon M.** *Student /Mentorship/Art Collector*

"I truly appreciate how Tonya provided ideas and thoughtful recommendations for business outreach and growth opportunities...She helped me transform my mind viruses to an eager, productive mindset... Even with the many obstacles that life brings, her encouragement, clear guidance, and support helped keep my business goals on track. I look forward to the continued business coaching and the fruitful journey ahead!"

—**Victoria E.** *Student-Art Marketing Mentorship/Art Collector*

"I am grateful to receive the work of a talented, insightful, and unique artist. Her work brings continuing inspiration and beauty. I am pleased to support her unique talent and gifts."

—**Angelamarie V.** *Art Collector*

"I purchased this as a gift for a friend. She LOVED it and was very impressed by the quality and insight of the reading and the artistry of the painting. The item exceeded my expectations, and the product descriptions are detailed and accurate. PaintingPoet quickly responded to all questions."

—**Sahedean** *Art Collector*

"You are nonjudgmental and are happy to give more knowledge or examples throughout."

—**Kathleen** *Student-Art Marketing Mentorship*

"The work is absolutely beautiful; I enjoy it every day I see it. Tonya is such a beautiful person. I'm so excited to have her paintings throughout my house."

—**Brenda W.** *Coaching/Art Collector*

"You are a "real" artist."

—**Susan S.** *Art Collector*

"I've experienced Tonya's energy portrait before and found her readings to be very accurate, she's the real deal with her healing and intuitive gifts. This spirit guide drawing was spot on and the message was fitting for the phase of my life I'm going through, it resonated. What's funny, I had recently did a meditation to contact my spirit animal and I blew it off b/c "I don't like birds" but sure enough... the crow showed up again and there's no way Tonya could've known that, so I know it's a real message. Thank you so much for sharing your gift."

—**Vanessa L.** *Art Collector*

Received this darling little painting quickly and very well-wrapped. It's a gift for a friend and it's perfect. Thank you!

—**Justy** *Art Collector*

# MOTIVATE AND INSPIRE OTHERS!
## "Share This Book"

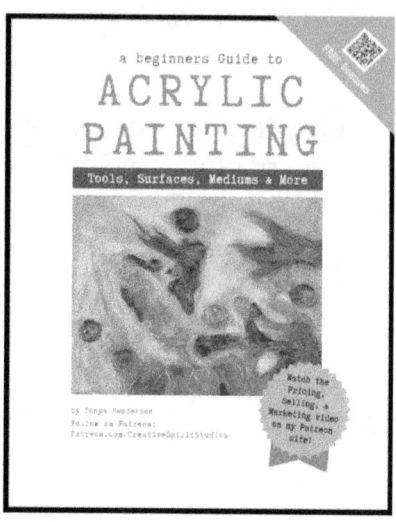

**Retail $14.95**
**Special Quantity Discounts**

| Quantity | Price |
|---|---|
| 5: 20 Books | $14.95 |
| 21: 99 Books | $12.95 |
| 100: 499 Books | $10.95 |
| 500: 999 Books | $9.95 |
| 1000 + Books | $7.95 |

**To Place an Order Contact**
**Creative Spirit Studios**
**810-471-0665**

# THE IDEAL PROFESSIONAL SPEAKER FOR YOUR NEXT EVENT!

Any organization that wants to help its people to become "extraordinary," needs to hire Tonya Henderson for a keynote and/or workshop training!

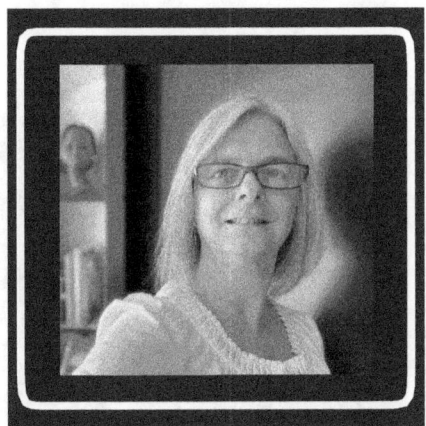

## TO CONTACT OR BOOK TONYA HENDERSON TO SPEAK:

Creative Spirit Studios LLC.
810-471-0665
Tonya-Henderson.com
Patreon.com/CreativeSpiritStudios

# THE IDEAL COACH/MENTOR FOR YOU!

If you're ready to overcome challenges, have breakthroughs,
and achieve higher levels, then you will love having Tonya Henderson as your coach and mentor!

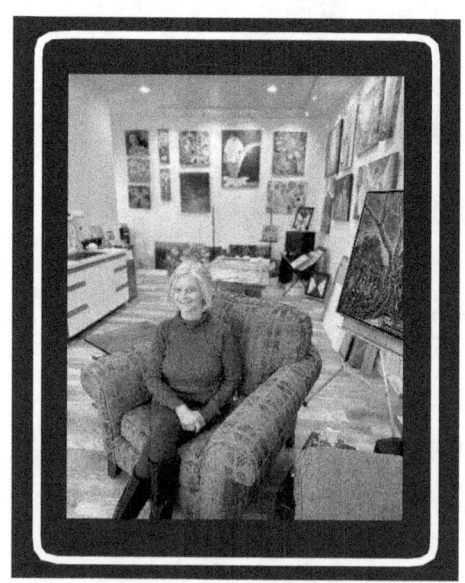

## TO CONTACT OR BOOK TONYA HENDERSON FOR COACHING:

Creative Spirit Studios LLC.
810-471-0665
Tonya-Henderson.com
Patreon.com/CreativeSpiritStudios

# DEDICATION

With heartfelt respect and deep gratitude, I dedicate this book to the extraordinary art teachers and instructors who have generously shared their time, talent, and wisdom with me throughout my journey.

From the Linden School District, Flint Institute of Art Museum Art School, to the Colorado Institute of Art and Dubner Training School, your passion for creativity and commitment to nurturing artistic expression have profoundly influenced my life. Each lesson and word of encouragement has not only enriched my skills but has also instilled in me a lasting appreciation for the transformative power of art.

Without your guidance, I would not be where I am today. Thank you for believing in me and inspiring countless others along the way. Your impact is truly immeasurable.

I would also like to extend a special thank you to Cheryl Murphy and the 1984-86 administration of the Colorado Institute of Art for your invaluable assistance in helping me find rideshare partners, housing, and additional funding. Your care and concern for my well-being made it possible for me to stay in Colorado and earn my degree. Thank you.

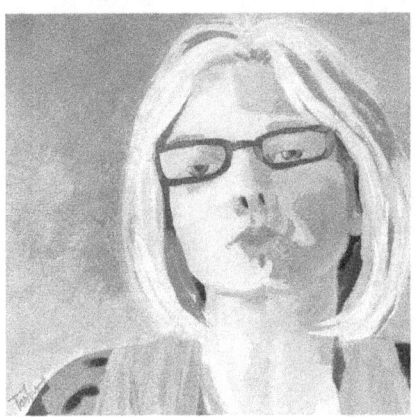

"Every artist dips his brush in his own soul. And paints his own nature into his pictures."
-- Vincent Van Gogh

# TABLE OF CONTENTS

| | |
|---|---|
| **INTRODUCTION** | **page 1** |
| **ACRYLIC PAINTING** | **page 3** |
| **ACRYLIC PAINT CHARACTERISTICS** | **page 4** |
| **ACRYLIC PAINT TYPES** | **page 6** |
| **ACRYLIC PAINT GRADES** | **page 8** |
| **ACRYLIC PAINTING SURFACES** | **page 10** |
| **PALETTES FOR ACRYLIC PAINTING** | **page 16** |
| **ACRYLIC PAINTING BRUSHES** | **page 20** |
| **ADDITIONAL PAINTING TOOLS** | **page 26** |
| **ACRYLIC GELS, MEDIUMS & PASTES** | **page 29** |
| **TERMINOLOGY: COLORS & PAINT** | **page 36** |
| **TERMINOLOGY: COMPOSITION** | **page 44** |
| **A BIT ABOUT COLOR** | **page 49** |
| **COLOR MIXING RECIPES** | **page 57** |
| **ADDITIONAL HELPFUL HINTS** | **page 65** |
| **ONE FINAL MESSAGE** | **page 68** |
| **ACKNOWLEDGMENTS** | **page 69** |
| **ABOUT THE AUTHOR** | **page 70** |
| **ADDITIONAL RESOURCES** | **page 72** |

# INTRODUCTION

I still remember the thrill of opening my first set of acrylic paints at around ten or twelve years old. It was the early 1970s, a time when acrylics were just beginning to carve out their place in the art world. Little did I know then that these vibrant colors would become a lifelong passion.

The story of acrylic paint begins in the 1930s when mineral-based pigments first emerged as house paint. It wasn't until 1953 that water-based acrylics became available to artists, gaining popularity in the 1960s with the introduction of modern high-viscosity formulas. In a way, I like to think that I grew up alongside these paints!

Back in 1972, I had no formal training in painting, but I eagerly experimented, mixing colors and applying them through trial and error. My journey led me to art school, where I discovered the joys of acrylics—*primarily due to the sensitivity many students had to oil paints.*

I thought I had an edge, but the truth is, I still had so much to learn. Even after graduating, and with decades of hindsight, I realize my understanding of painting was just beginning.

In the 1980s, acrylics were still relatively new, and resources were scarce—no internet or Google to provide guidance. I was creating work that seemed to resonate with others, yet I often felt a lingering sense of inadequacy, as if my art wasn't truly "good enough."

A feeling that I'm sure many of you have felt or soon will if you are undergoing your own discovery of acrylic painting.

Today, I'm proud to say I'm a more accomplished painter, thanks to years of practice, teaching others, and the simple act of creating. Over the past 15 years alone, I've produced anywhere from two to three hundred paintings each year!

While I hesitate to call myself an expert, I can share that I've spent 50 years creating art with acrylics and 24 years teaching it. Along the way, I've learned valuable lessons that I hope will help you navigate your own trial-and-error journey more efficiently.

In this book, I want to give you the terminology and basic information about the paint, tools, surfaces, and more, that was so lacking when I started painting.

If you're eager to dive deeper into the acrylic painting process through videos and "Ask Me Anything" sessions, I invite you to join me on Patreon at the Artsy Spirit level.

Together, we can make your learning experience even more enjoyable and fulfilling. You can find me at **Patreon.com/CreativeSpiritStudios** where I will give you all I can to speed up your journey to becoming a full-fledged acrylic painter!

I'm truly grateful you're here, and I hope the insights in this book help you unleash your creativity and find joy in your artistic journey!

# ACRYLIC PAINTING

Acrylic paint is permanently flexible, durable, and water-resistant when dry. It can even serve as an adhesive, making it suitable for collage work. As a water-based paint, it can be thinned with water and easily cleaned up with soap and water.

One of the standout features of acrylic paint is its quick drying time. Thin layers can dry within 10 to 20 minutes; however, they may only be dry to the touch. A "skin" will form on the outer layer while the underlying paint may remain wet for several hours or even days.

Acrylics are permanent and lightfast, comparable to oils, and in some ways, they may even outperform them. Only time will tell, as acrylics are a relatively newer medium, having been introduced to the market in the mid to late 20th century.

**The following information will help you learn the basics of the products you may need as you embark on your painting adventure.**

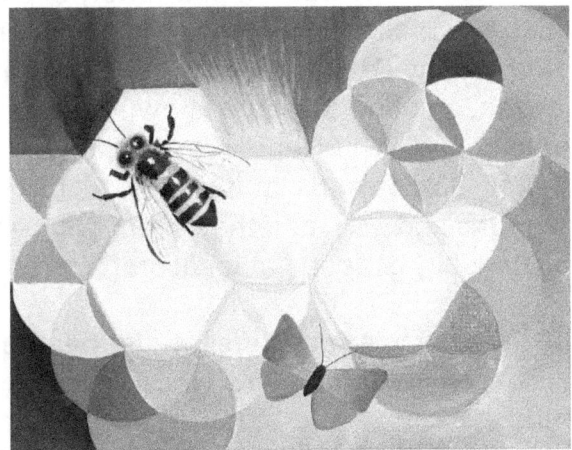

# ACRYLIC PAINT CHARACTERISTICS

Acrylic paint is a combination of pigment, polymer emulsion, and water. As the water evaporates, the pigments remain suspended within the dry polymer, causing the mixture to shrink and darken in color. Once dry, acrylics become permanent, flexible, and water-resistant, resisting cracking and discoloration.

Acrylic paints are versatile and can be used in various ways to mimic both watercolor and oil painting. They dry rapidly, allowing for quick overpainting. However, drying time can vary depending on factors such as the type of paint, its consistency, the thickness of application, the humidity, and the surface you are working on. It's important to note that the surface may feel dry to the touch, while layers underneath remain wet. Generally, acrylic paint requires a curing time of 24 to 48 hours to dry completely.

Many paint companies offer a variety of paint consistencies, which can make it challenging for beginners to select the right product. Brands like Liquitex, Golden, Winsor & Newton, and Sennelier are known for their professional-grade colors. While there are many other options on the market, Golden and Liquitex provide the largest selection of mediums and gels, and they, along with Winsor & Newton, can typically be found at local craft stores.

These companies also offer student-grade paint, which is a less expensive option for those just beginning their artistic journey. It is essential to consider your goals when selecting paint. If you are pursuing a career as a professional painter, investing in the best paint your budget allows is advisable. Professional-grade paints typically have a higher pigment load, and you may need to adjust your mixing techniques when transitioning from student-grade products.

Student-grade paint is excellent for beginners or those who will paint only as a hobby. However, I do not recommend small craft bottles for serious students, except for tole painting. These bottles contain more binder and water and less pigment, which reduces costs. Cheap paint isn't better paint; however, their consistency makes them perfect for decorative painting projects.

You may notice a wet-to-dry color shift when painting with acrylics. Until recently, this was common across all brands. However, Winsor & Newton has developed a new polymer base that reduces this effect, making it easier to match color mixtures. Liquitex has also adopted this new technology, and other companies will likely follow suit soon.

In the next section, you will find descriptions that can help you select the appropriate paint for your chosen project. Keep in mind that any acrylic product can be combined with any other acrylic product in various mixing or layering combinations. However, the following products should only be used specifically for their intended purposes:

- **Gesso:** A primer best used alone; thick applications may crack.
- **Varnish:** A removable final coat.
- **Additives:** Must be used correctly, as they do not contain a binder.

# ACRYLIC PAINT TYPES

**Soft Body:** A versatile paint that is creamy and smooth. The original professional acrylic paint with a heavy cream consistency.

**Heavy Body:** These are thicker, more like toothpaste, and spread like butter. Heavy body paint is excellent for heavy paint applications where textures are desirable, such as knife painting or oil painting techniques.

**Super Heavy Body:** Excellent for textural or sculptural applications with low shrinkage and increased open time for easier blending. Superior shape retention and will hold super-high peaks and knife marks.

**Fluid Acrylic:** These paints are very thin and pourable. They are also very highly pigmented paints and are recommended for watercolor techniques.

**Open Acrylics:** These are creamy and have a slightly longer dry time.

**Interference Colors:** These are colorless and transparent colors produced with mica flakes rather than pigments. They exhibit a metallic look and color shift depending on the way the light hits. They will be labeled as Opalescent colors.

**Iridescent Colors:** These produce a variety of metallic effects. Made from titanium-coated mica flakes and containing a light-absorbing colorant. They are optically opaque and rely on reflected light. There is no flip of color as with the Interference colors.

**Fluorescent Colors:** These are intense and brilliant colors with a lightfastness rating of III. They are fun to work with but are not meant for professional permanent work. They are created with dyes that absorb light and reflect a longer light wave resulting in their fluorescent glow.

**Airbrush Acrylics:** These are the consistency of ink, thin and watery. They are designed to move through an airbrush without further dilution.

**Craft Paints:** These paints are specifically formulated for tole painting or decorative painting and require no further dilution for these techniques. They will dry to a matte finish.

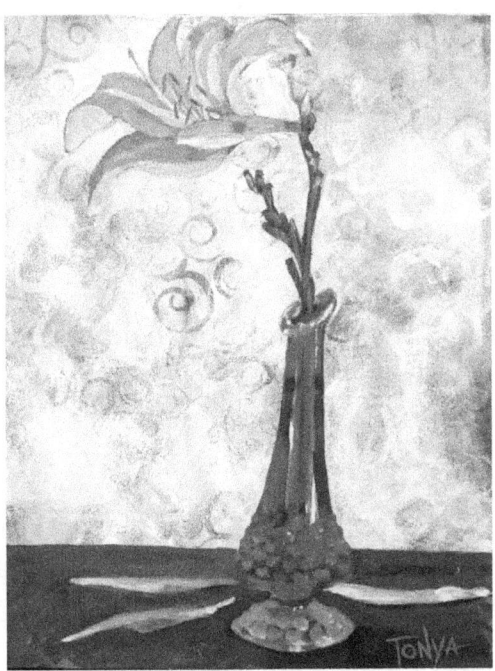

# ACRYLIC PAINT GRADES

Acrylic paint comes in three grades which are created for different types of painters. If you are a hobby painter, you won't require the best quality paint. If you want to become a professional painter, you may very well want to use professional quality paint. Knowing the difference between the grades can help you select a paint grade that will serve you well.

Below I'll describe the grades and explain why you might want to use each of them based on how experienced you might be and what you plan on doing with your work once it's been created.

**Three Paint Grades:**

**Professional-Grade:** These paints have the highest pigment content and dry to a gloss finish. They are the best choice for the professional artist.

**Student-Grade:** These paints contain more fillers and less pigment. They are an excellent choice for students, hobbyists, and those venturing into the professional marketplace.

**Craft-Grade:** These contain the most filler, less pigment, and tend to dry matte. These are excellent for crafting projects, tole painting, and decorative painting techniques.

All acrylic paints, whether they are typical tube paints, heavy body, professional, or student grade, are mixable with one another. Never be afraid to mix a fluid color with a heavy medium and use it in a fashion it may not have been created for. Acrylic paint is acrylic paint, period.

These different types of paint were created to make certain techniques easier to achieve without the use of additives or mediums. When choosing which paint grade is correct for you, first decide what painting technique you would like to learn and then choose the paint that will make that technique the easiest for you to accomplish.

**If in doubt, choose a student-grade** tube paint at your local craft store. These paints can be thinned for watercolor, tole painting, and decorative painting techniques, as well as thickened for texture, knife painting, and oil painting techniques. There is no need to purchase high-end professional colors unless you intend to think of yourself as a professional rather than a hobbyist.

(The time to shift paint grade is once you have decided to start showing your work in galleries. At this point it would serve you well to upgrade to professional-level supplies.)

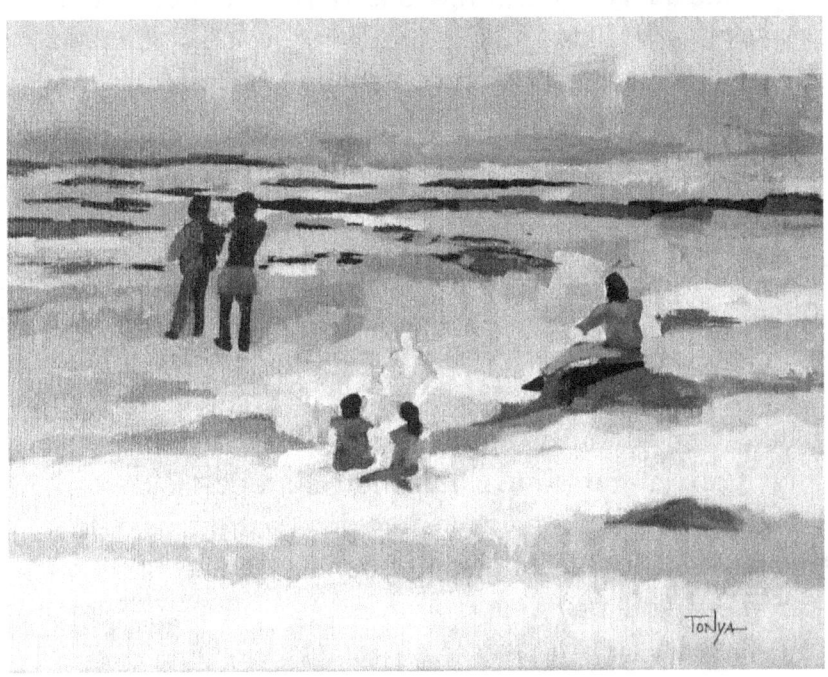

# ACRYLIC PAINTING SURFACES

The surfaces suitable for acrylic painting are varied and numerous, allowing for a wide range of materials to be painted. However, some surfaces may require a primer or medium to enhance adhesion. The following information will give you a basic understanding of how to work with this diverse selection of surfaces.

**Acrylic paint has excellent adhesion to most painting surfaces. Achieve the best results by preparing your surfaces properly.**

**Unfinished Wood:** Base your decision to paint on wood projects on your desired result. Although wood does not require a primer, it may be desirable to use a primer if the entire piece is painted, if it will be used outdoors, or if it will be an object that will be handled frequently. I have achieved nice results using a wall primer such as KILZ or Benz when trying to cover or hide knots, although I have also used gesso as a primer for smaller projects. Sealing with a varnish may also be desirable, especially if the item will be handled often or is for the outdoors.

**Finished Wood:** Painting on finished wood requires careful consideration, especially if the surface is coated with varnish. While it is possible to paint over varnished surfaces, the paint may not adhere well and may not last overtime. Acrylic paint can be effectively applied to stained wood. Typically, you should sand the area to be painted and use a primer if you intend to cover the entire surface. However, primer is not always necessary for spot illustrations or for items that will not be handled frequently. Once your painting is complete, you may wish to protect the surface. For small wooden objects, I usually use an acrylic spray sealer, while larger items can be varnished. For furniture, I prefer a rub-on polyurethane finish.

**Metal:** Although metal may be a challenge, it is paintable! However, it's critical that you thoroughly clean the metal before you begin. This could mean a rinse with a damp rag or a process of cleaning with denatured alcohol to prepare the surface. Once the cleaning has been completed, give the item a day or so to dry completely, and then use a metal primer to create a great painting surface.

**Glass:** Glass can also be tricky, but doable! It too will need to be cleaned well before you begin. First, wash it with soap and water and allow it to dry. Before applying paint, be sure to wipe the area to be painted with rubbing alcohol to remove potential fingerprints, as they repel the paint. Also, be sure to purchase the proper paint or glass painting medium to help you be more successful. You can find these at your local craft store.

**Fabric:** Acrylic paints are suitable for painting a variety of fabric types. You will want to consider your project before purchasing your paint selection.

- **Wearable Items:** You can use any acrylic paint to paint on fabric; however, if you plan to paint wearable items, it's advisable to choose paint specifically designed for this purpose. These specialized paints contain additives that enhance softness and flexibility, making them less stiff. Keep in mind that applying multiple layers of paint can reduce the overall flexibility of the fabric, so it's best to keep designs simple and graphic to maintain flexibility.

- **Outdoor cloth:** Consider a primer and a sealer for anything you paint upon that will be exposed to the elements. This will increase its longevity, as paint wears quickly when exposed to the weather. Any acrylics will work for these projects; however, you may want to consider a fabric paint for flexibility or an outdoor line that may increase longevity.
- **Handbags Etc.:** Fabric items, such as handbags and chair seats, can also be successfully painted. I often update vintage bags with a modern touch by simply adding a painted design. In this case, I typically forgo both primer and sealer. However, if you prefer to use a sealer, I recommend opting for a spray.

**Paper:** Acrylic paint can be successfully used on any type of paper. However, keep in mind that thinner paper may curl, so it's advisable to use less water with your paint applications or opt for heavier cardstock. While sealing the paper beforehand is an option, it is not necessary.

It will be helpful to know that paper draws moisture from your brush more rapidly than other paint surfaces and may require you to dip into the paint more often to keep consistent in your brushwork. Once a layer of paint has been applied it becomes more like painting on other surfaces.

**Watercolor Paper:** This type of paper comes in two finishes: a smooth finish known as Hot Press and a rough finish called Cold Press. It is available in a wide range of weights, from lightweight 140 lb. paper to heavyweight 400 lb. paper. Watercolor paper can be found in sheets or blocks, with blocks being particularly convenient as they eliminate the need for taping down or stretching. While this paper does not require a primer, you can use gesso to seal and prime it if desired. When using watercolor paper for acrylics, keep in mind that each layer of acrylic applied makes the paper less absorbent.

- **Lightweight Paper Sheets:** This paper must be stretched before painting. Wet it well on both sides and secure it on a board with wide gummed tape. The tape should be placed so that half covers the paper while the other half secures the paper to the board. Allow the paper to air-dry thoroughly. This can be avoided by purchasing your paper in blocks.
- **Heavyweight Paper Sheets:** Tape to a board on all edges to keep the paper from warping or curling. No stretching is required for heavier-weight papers. Although you can adhere it for stability.

**Canvas Panels:** Canvas panels often come with a surface that may repel paint. I recommend you use gesso to seal and prime before painting on this surface. I have even been known to wash the surface with soap and water to increase adhesion before applying the gesso.

**Canvas Paper:** Canvas paper can be a fun alternative to regular paper or canvas products. It too, however, can have a replant surface quality or be too absorbent and it may serve you well to put a coat of gesso on before painting.

**Rolled Canvas:** Rolled canvas can be great for painting and mounting to a wall. It's often used for stretching your own canvas surfaces, or by those who ship large paintings, as they can be stretched on bars once received. I have used large, rolled canvas products for painting floorcloths as well. Rolled canvas comes primed or unprimed. If you stretch your own and you have purchased an unprimed canvas, it is recommended that you stretch first and then prime with two or three coats of gesso before painting.

**Stretched Canvas:** Stretched canvas can be found in a variety of fabrics, brands, and quality choices. There are so many options to choose from, it can be difficult to make your selection. Use the following recommendation to assist you.

- **Bulk packages are great for beginners:** and practice but are very low quality and can make painting more challenging than it needs to be. As a rule, always choose the best canvas you can afford. Cotton is a good choice and comes in a variety of weights and textures. Linen canvases are considered the most desirable and highest quality canvases. (By "bulk" I mean packages containing five or more canvases found at craft stores, as it is quite possible to purchase good canvases in bulk, they are however still packaged for sale individually)
- **Student Grade Canvas:** is better than bulk canvases as the weave of the fabric is much tighter and the threads are much thicker.
- **Studio Grade Canvas:** is better than student grade with thicker threads and a tighter weave.
- **Professional Grade Canvas:** can mean cotton or linen fabric. Remember that better quality fabric tends to be darker in value and better fabric usually means better stretcher bars.

**Wood Cradles:** Cradles are a great choice for those who like to paint with heavy applications of both paint and/or mediums and holds up well to the weight of thick, layered painting techniques.

**Masonite:** This is a pressed wood board that is smooth on one side and rough on the other. It can be found and cut at your local lumber yard. This surface is typically coated with Gesso primer before painting and can be painted on either side. It is a great choice for attaching objects, or heavier applications of paint or mediums.

**Illustration Board:** This is a paper-coated cardboard that comes in two surface textures, a hot-pressed smooth surface or a cold-pressed textured surface. The paper coating is of high quality and these boards resemble a mat board in density and structure. They require no additional stretching or support, can be primed or not primed, and are suitable for matting and framing. They are not recommended for heavy paint applications and may curl with excess water.

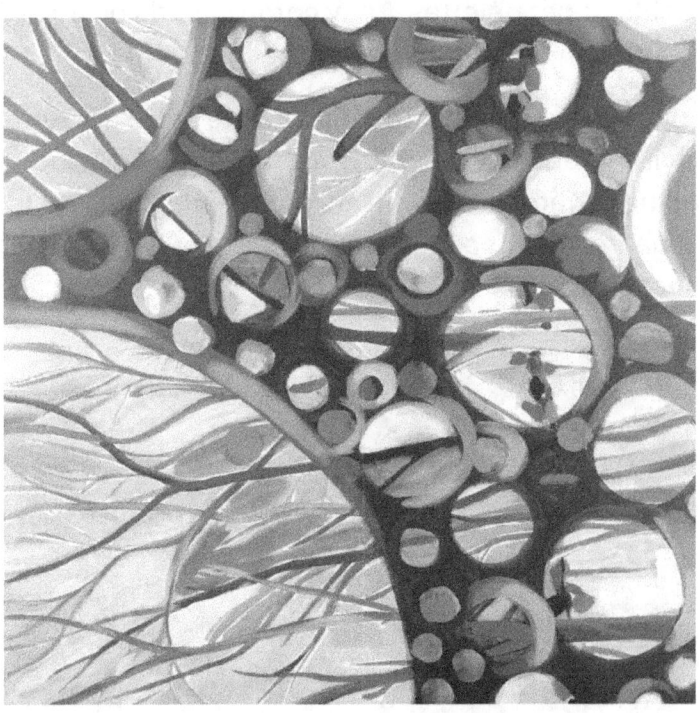

# PALETTES FOR ACRYLIC PAINTING

Choose a painting palette based on whether you are working on a single project, are a beginning student, or want to make painting a regular hobby or full-time career.

It doesn't make sense to purchase anything special if you have a one-time project and have something like leftover ceramic tiles in your garage, or a piece of framing glass sitting around. Both of these surfaces will work fine as a temporary palette. If you don't have one of these items lying around, instead, use a foam dinner plate.

In addition, you certainly don't want to carry a piece of tile or glass back and forth from your home workspace to a classroom situation either. In this case, pick up some disposable paper palettes. They come in pads on 40 or 50 sheets and can be found at your local hobby or craft store.

At home, however, use something a little more cost-effective and environmentally friendly. If you are a painting enthusiast or heading toward a career in acrylic painting be sure to pick up an enamel tray or a stay-wet palette. I believe these are your best choices.

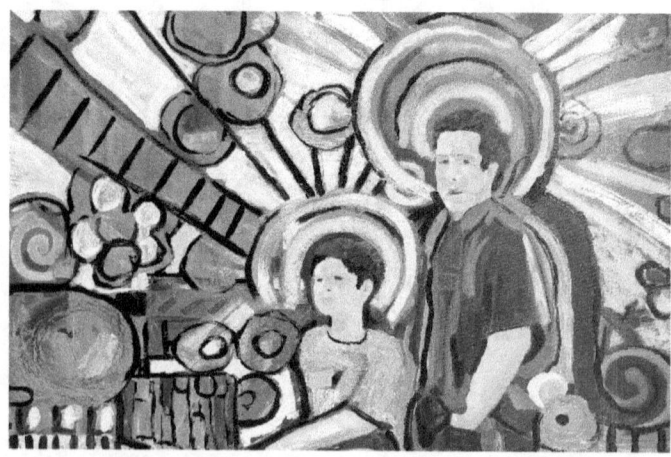

**Make your selection from the following list based on your needs.**

**Enameled Butcher Trays:** This is my first choice in a palette for multiple reasons. It is non-absorbent, non-stick with acrylic paint, and comes with raised edges to keep the wet paint contained. They come in a variety of sizes to suit your needs.

**Ceramic Tile:** These can be a good choice to use as a palette if you happen to have a nice 12x12-inch piece sitting out in your garage. Some work better than others, so try them out if you have them. These are not as slick as the enameled tray or a sheet of glass but can work for you. It has no edge, so it's not a good choice for fluid painting techniques.

**Picture Glass:** Although this is an excellent choice for a non-absorbent, non-stick surface to use as a palette, they have their drawbacks. Be sure to tape the edges so that you don't slice a finger and securely place it on your work surface to ensure it is not dropped! Again, this surface has no edges and therefore is not a good choice for wetter, more fluid painting techniques.

**Plexiglass:** This is a great palette when thick and heavy. It is non-absorbent, non-stick, and won't slice your fingers or break when it hits the floor. However, there are no edges unless you have one specially made for you!

**Formica:** I have never tried this, I am however, aware that it is much like working with glass. If you have it, use it, but if you are going to buy something, consider the enamel tray instead.

**Wooden Palette:** A wooden palette is generally coated to make for a slicker surface and can be used for acrylic painting. These, however, are not the best choice for acrylic painting. The surface coat can wear off leaving your paint to stick. Many wooden palettes are meant for oil painting.

**Plastic Palette**: Small round molded plastic trays are available at every hobby shop, but I would prefer to use almost anything else—such as a sheet of wax paper—before resorting to one of these. They can easily become stained by paint pigments, and once paint dries on them, it can be nearly impossible to remove! I recommend saving them for watercolors or simply throwing them away.

**Stay Wet Palette:** These plastic trays have a unique twist: they feature a moistened sponge at the bottom, which is covered by special paper, and they come with a lid. The sides of the tray help contain the paint, preventing it from running off the edges, while keeping it slightly moister for a longer period. You can cover the tray and return later to find the paint still wet. Although these trays are useful, they are not magical! Your paints will eventually dry out, as they are not typically airtight; it just takes longer. These trays can be a good choice if you understand their limitations.

**Disposable Paper:** These are wax-coated paper palettes that can be tossed away after use. They are a good choice for classroom use but not my first choice for studio painting. Think environmentally and choose something that will last you year to year. It will be better for your budget as well.

**Styrofoam Plate or Tray:** These can be a great choice for those with a one-time project in mind or for use in the classroom. They are non-absorbent, unlike paper plates which dry your paint out too quickly. They keep the paint moist and are readily available, and disposable. These of course are horrible for the environment, so stick to something reusable when possible.

**Palette Care:** A little tip for keeping your enameled tray or slick surface palette clean is to wipe away leftover wet paint with a paper towel. If your paint has dried on the palette, use a hand-held single-sided razor blade scraper, to scrap away larger chunks. Then pour a little bit of hot water on your palette and let it sit for just a few seconds to a minute. You will see the paint begin to lift off the palette, as soon as this occurs, remove the water and wipe with a paper towel to remove loosened paint. You will want to keep the paint particles from going down your drain or attaching to your sink surface, so be sure not to let the water sit on your palette too long. Be sure to check out my videos on my off-loading technique to save you both time and money! You may find one on my YouTube channel or subscribe to my Patreon page at **Patreon.com/CreativeSpiritStudios**

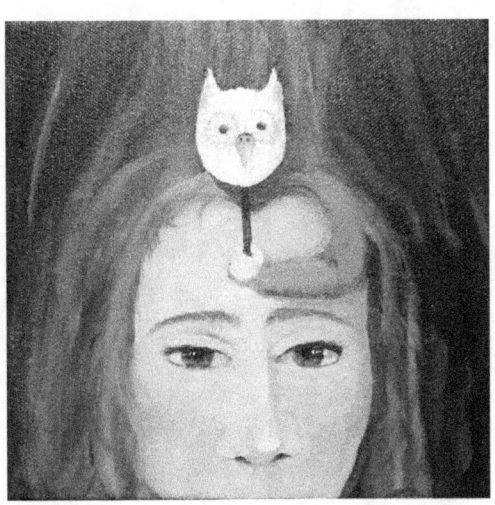

# ACRYLIC PAINTING BRUSHES

With such a large variety of brushes and brush makers, it can be challenging to figure out what you need to have as a beginning painter.

I have found that I can be rather rough on my brushes and prefer to purchase good quality, moderately priced brushes and replace them more often. I can say that the cheapest brushes are cheap for a reason. They do not perform as a better-quality brush would, and they do not last but for a hot minute.

They tend to lose bristles and can cause many headaches when those bristles end up on your paint surface.

If you are just going to give this painting thing a try, a cheap brush might do the trick for you. Disposable brushes are great for one-off projects.

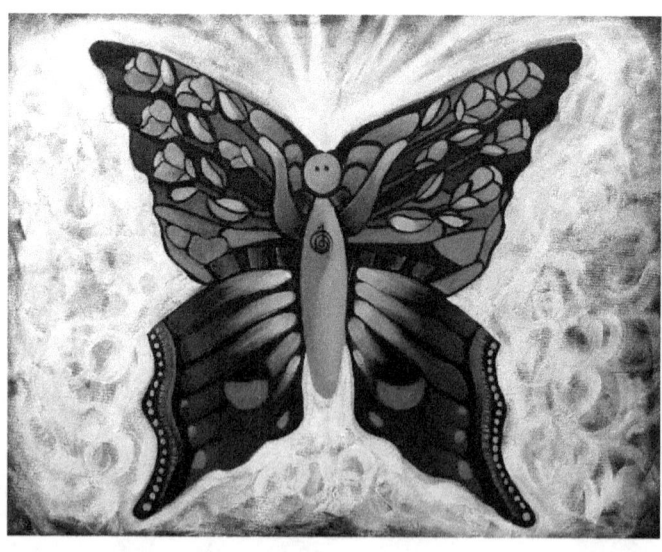

However, if you think you might stick with it for a while, spend a little extra money on a better brush. Painting with a cheap brush is like trying to learn to play the guitar with a child's toy. It just won't serve you well.

I would also like to point out that most of my painting is done with a bright, flat, or round brush. It's nice to have a few other brushes around and I have several others... okay, a lot of others... but I typically only pull out the other brushes for very specific purposes, and this does not happen as often as you might think.

**I don't recommend you purchase too many specialty brushes in the beginning. No matter how cool they are!**

It might serve you way better to bring home a foam brush, the kind you can find at both the craft store and the hardware store, and a super wide flat brush for glazing and gradations before you invest in a rake or a fan. There are many more specialty brushes that unless you get into highly detailed work or tole painting are simply not necessary.

Decorative painting and tole painting are where my recommendations might change. Because they utilize specific brushes to create stroke work that requires them.

Watch some videos or take a few classes to see understand which brush is recommended and how to use them, rather than looking at all the brushes and thinking how cool they look. It might be better to spend your extra dollars on more paint or additional paint surfaces!

**Brush Types -**

- **Flat:** long bristles that lay flat on your surface and come to a flat tip.
- **Bright:** like a flat with shorter bristles. My go-to brush.
- **Filbert:** a rounded corner flat brush excellent for flower petals and curved edges.
- **Round:** a pointed brush used for details and tight spaces.
- **Liner:** like a round only smaller and with fewer bristles, used to create fine lines such as branches, grass, and eyelashes.
- **Long Liner:** a liner with extra-long bristles, used for long sweeping strokes like vines or lettering.
- **Rigger:** A long round slender pointed sable brush. For fine lines.
- **Rake:** cut with gaps between the bristles for grass and fur.

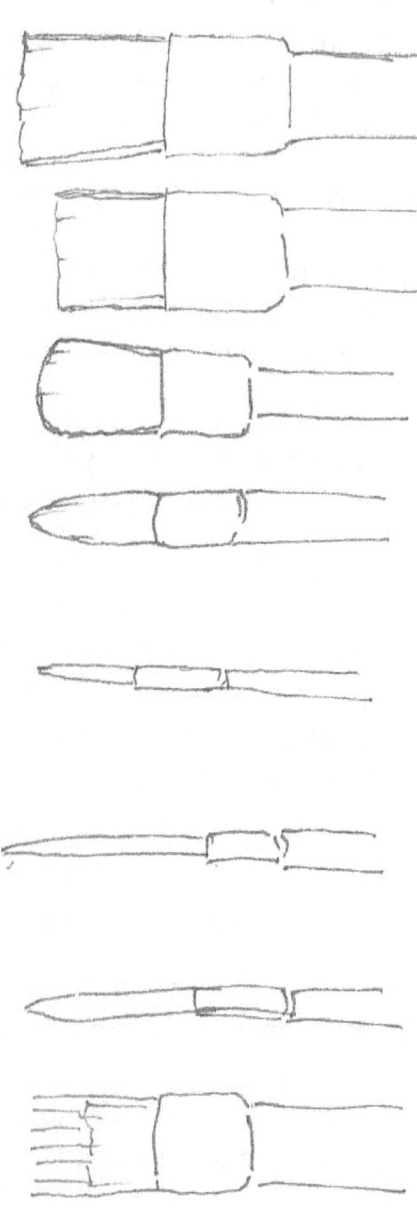

- **Fan:** bristles are long and in the shape of a fan, used to create texture or to blend.
- **Scruffy:** looks like a cross between a flat and a round. The ferrule is typically flattened and bristles flair like a round that has been cut off producing a flat surface area. These brushes were created to mimic an old worn-out flat brush which is excellent for creating texture and stippling techniques.
- **Deerfoot:** a round brush with a flat angled surface rather than a point, used for creating fur, bushes, etc.
- **Sponge:** large and flat with a chisel. Cover large areas quickly without leaving brush marks.
- **Chisel Edge:** the flat tip of a flat or bright brush, used to create lines.
- **Ferrule:** the metal part of the brush that holds the bristles in place.

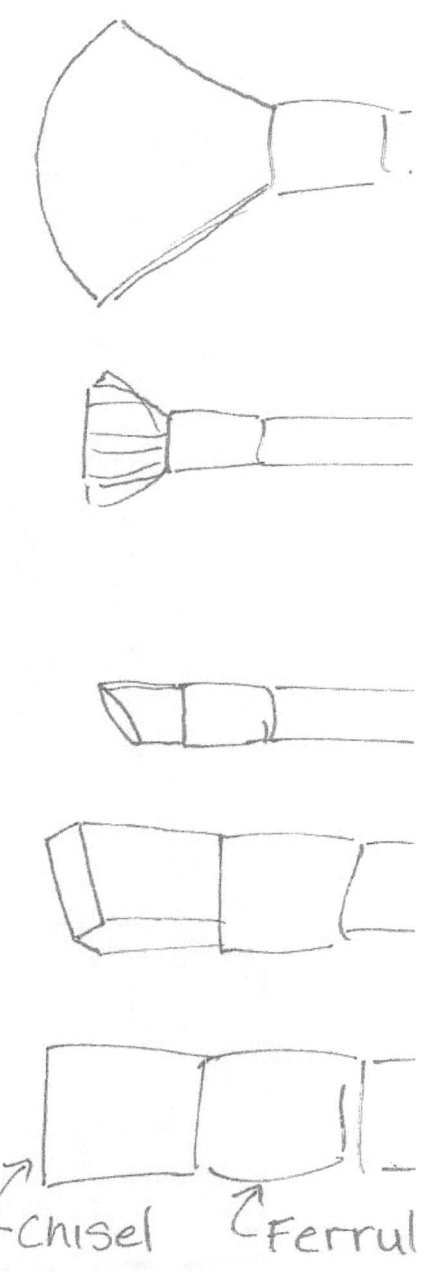

- **Bristle:** these brushes are great for heavier thicker paint applications.
- **Synthetic:** these brushes are best for thinner, smoother paint applications.

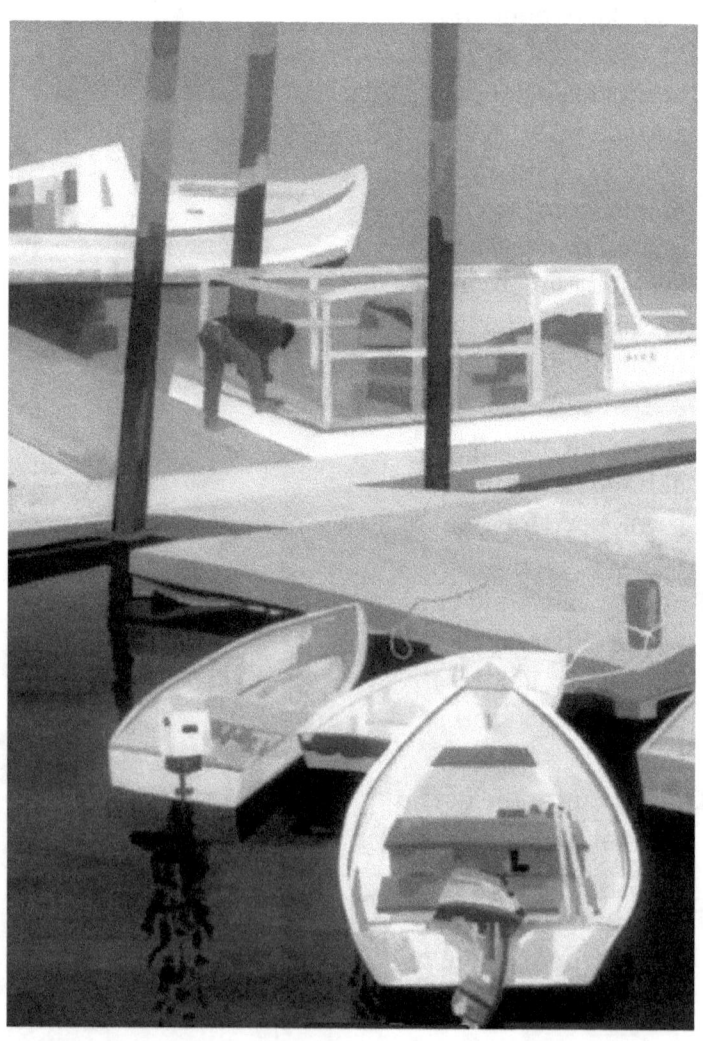

**Brush care:**

As acrylic paint is essentially plastic, they can ruin a brush in as little as ten minutes when left with paint on the bristles. It is recommended you **never lay a brush down without thoroughly rinsing first.**

Brushes should be cleaned properly at the end of each paint session with soap and water to remove any remaining pigment, and dried lying flat. There are specialty cleaning products for brushes, but I would rather have an extra tube of paint with my dollar and use the hand soap I already own.

This is my preference, others may disagree. Remember, I use moderately priced brushes so that I may replace them more often.

If you utilize a jar or vertical container for storage of your brushes, be sure your brushes are dried thoroughly before storing them. Any paint pigments remaining on the brush will fall into the area below and near the ferrule, become hardened, and shorten the life of your brush. But hey, that's how we create our own scruffy brushes!

Brushes should never be left in a water container or at an angle on the palette, as the bristles can begin to curl. It is recommended that they lay flat on your work surface, preferably with moistened bristles while in a painting session.

Always use lukewarm to cool water when cleaning your brushes and in your water containers, as hot water can soften and loosen the glue holding your bristles in.

# ADDITIONAL PAINTING TOOLS

**Hair Dryer:** A hair dryer can become a very useful tool for acrylic painters. It allows you to dry your paint layer much quicker for speedier overpainting. Don't be fooled by a dry-to-the-touch paint surface however, acrylic paint will need a 24 to 48-hour dry time to cure completely.

**Spray Bottle:** Everyone should have a spray bottle nearby! Spray a fine mist over your colors on the palette to keep them moist and prolong the inevitable skinning over of your colors! The spray bottle is also handy if you are using paint color from a jar, simply spray a mist over the top of the paint inside before recapping, this helps prevent the paint from drying out. I also use the spray bottle to keep the painting surface moist and for certain painting techniques.

**Scraping Tools:** I keep a variety of tools on hand that can be used for scraping, such as wide plastic scrapers, rubber tip scrapers, old credit cards, or nails. There are a variety of new products on the market that look like fun for scraping techniques or you can use your imagination and create your own.

**Palette Knife:** A palette knife is an excellent tool for getting paint out of jars and mixing colors on your palette. In addition, you can use it for scraping or painting.

**Painting Knives & Spatulas:** Mix color and manipulate textures using these tools. They are specially designed to spread color directly on your painting surface. If you are interested in knife painting techniques invest in high-quality knives and spatulas as they may indeed last a lifetime. I have some that I purchased as a teen, and have worn two so thin they have broken, the others are still in usable condition nearly 40 years later.

**Sponges:** These tools are handy for applying or removing paint. I keep a variety of sizes, shapes, and textures. Sea sponges are super nice but don't discount the sponges you may have around the house already. I use kitchen sponges, and cosmetic sponges and look for scraps of upholstery foam at the local fabric store. All work in a similar fashion and each gives a slightly different texture.

**Rags & Paper Towels:** This is a must-have, and not just for spills and messes! You will need rags and paper towels for a variety of techniques, to keep your brushes clean as you work, and for creating textures.

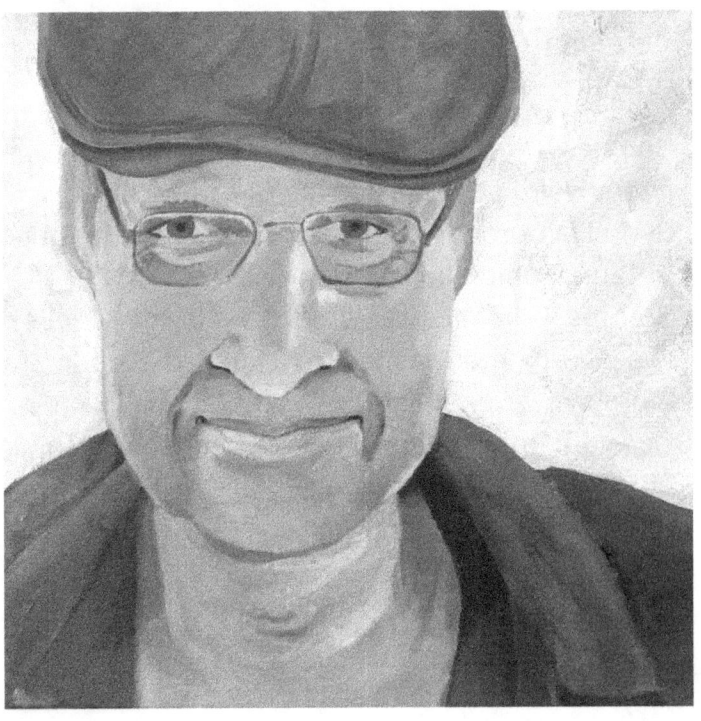

**Water Containers:** Another must-have! Use anything you have, to keep water handy as you paint. It is preferable to have two containers of water available as you paint. One for cleaning the brush and the other for providing clean water to mix with paint. I love to use handmade pottery for my water containers, but I always keep around the plastic deli containers for transporting to and from the classroom. You could also use coffee mugs or yogurt containers.

**Hand-Held Scraper Blade:** This little tool will save you a lot of time scraping paint from your butcher tray palette. It will work on your glass, ceramic, and other palettes as well, just remember that some surfaces don't take scraping with a razor blade as well as others!

And if you want to indulge your lurking experimental scientist side try painting with things like:

- Bubble wrap
- Other weird shaped, packaging materials
- Stencils (purchase at a craft store or make your own)
- Potato or onion bag netting
- Stamps (purchase at a craft store or make your own) I've glued metal washers to a block of wood!
- A brayer
- Use your imagination with other household things like curlers or a drywall trowel.

# ACRYLIC GELS, MEDIUMS & PASTES

Every year it seems there are more and more of these products to choose from, and it becomes more and more difficult to keep them all straight. So here are a few tips that will help you make your selection from the multitude of products available.

First, **you don't need any of these things** to get started painting with acrylics!

I hope this will ease your mind before you begin to read the list below. 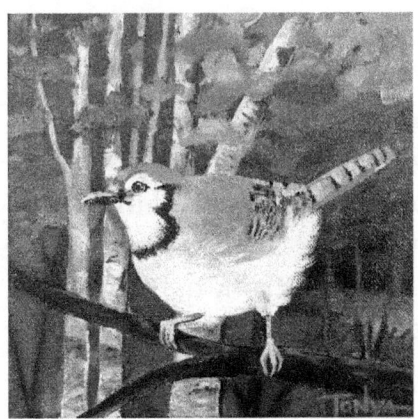 For a beginner, it might be a wise thing to get to know your paint qualities and a few painting techniques before you invest in a collection of products that may sit on the shelf and harden before you get a clear understanding of what they are used for.

When I first started painting with acrylics, matte medium, gloss medium, and gesso were the extras. Since that time, other products have come on the market to make the work of techniques easier for the artists, and to introduce new techniques to the public.

It is important to realize that acrylic painting hasn't been around that long. They were first created in the 1940s as mineral spirit-based paints and then introduced commercially in the 1950s, first as house paints. In 1955 Liquitex developed water-based, soft body paints for the artist. Heavy body paints were not available until the early

1960s! Many painters wouldn't touch this new paint at that time. It was considered too bright and gosh, they were for the student, not the professional painter.

Things have changed considerably since the 1950's. Artists have begun to experiment, push boundaries, and move into new territory with acrylic painting.

As new ideas and techniques developed so did new products. These products are designed to make techniques easier to accomplish. So, it is best to **understand the techniques and pick and choose your products** based on what you are trying to achieve.

With that knowledge under your belt, some of the most useful products may still **be matte and gloss mediums, gesso, and varnishes**. Here is why. Professional-grade acrylics have a nice glossy sheen to them. Some of the less expensive paints will be more matte and the cheap craft paints will be very matte. As you paint with any of these and add water to thin them, they become less glossy and more matte.

If you like that matte finish you may want to add the matte medium to your paint in place of water to thin. If you like the glossier finish, you may want to use the gloss medium to thin your paint. In either case, you can use the medium to coat your painting to shift the finish at any time during the painting process. You can also blend these two mediums to create any degree of satin finish you desire. It is recommended that you do not dilute your acrylic paint more than 25%-30% with water, further dilution can be accomplished by utilizing a matte or gloss type medium. I recommend staying under 25% as guessing these ratios can be a bit tricky.

**Gesso:** can be used on multiple surfaces to create a suitable ground for painting, making it a useful product, and perhaps one of the first a new student should invest in. Remember that it is a primer and not meant for mixing with paint.

**Varnish:** is a great way to finish off a completed painting. Giving it a nice non-porous surface and making cleaning of the painting surface easier. It is good to know, however, that it is not as necessary to varnish acrylic paintings as it is to varnish oil paintings. This is a step that could be skipped as acrylic painting has completely different properties than oil painting.

As a general point of reference, **gels are typically thinner and dry clear,** whereas a **paste will have an additional body and typically dries opaque**. These mediums, gels, and pastes contain no pigment and can be added to any acrylic paint grade and used in any combination of layering.

This list will give you general guidance for a wide variety of products. It may not, however, be a complete list of all products, as so many new products are being produced as we discover new properties and develop new techniques for their use.

**Clear Leveling Gel or Self Leveling Gel:** This is a thick stringy consistency gel, with high gloss and fluidity. Designed to produce an even film with excellent clarity. It can be used for glazes.

**Soft Gel:** Thinner than Heavy Body colors, moderately pourable, holds only slight peaks, transparent. Ideal for glazing or use as an isolation coat (thin 2:1). Available in gloss, matte, and semi-gloss.

**Regular Gel:** Extends paint and holds peaks and textures. Creamy thick consistency like Heavy Body colors. Available as gloss, matte, or semi-gloss.

**Heavy Gel:** Thicker, holds peaks, translucent. Use to alter sheen, increase paint body, extend color, and increase translucency. Available as gloss, matte, or semi-gloss.

**Extra Heavy Gel:** Very thick, holds peaks, dries translucent, and ideal for impasto techniques. Available in gloss, matte, semi-gloss.

**(MIX) Extra Heavy Gel & Molding Paste:** Increases viscosity, semi-opaque. Use to build surfaces.

**High Solid Gel:** Thickest of the gels. Holds high peaks and retains tool marks. Contains less water, shrinking less than other gels. Use to simulate oil paint. Available in gloss and matte.

**Clear Granular Gel:** Clear, coarse-textured granular solids, adds texture without altering color. Rough crushed glass appearance.

**Glass Bead Gel:** Clear with densely packed glass beads. Adds texture and a luminous effect.

**Clear Tar Gel:** Stringy, tar-like, and transparent. This gel is excellent for using with drip techniques. Let it sit after mixing to allow foam bubbles to rise, then pour.

**Pumice Gel:** Coarse or Fine. Coarse dries opaque grey and textural like concrete. Fine dries to a toothy grey, excellent for mixed media techniques.

**Fiber Paste:** Creates a rough, flexible, paper-like surface. Use as a ground or for texture.

**Molding Paste:** Extra heavy, off-white, semi-opaque, semi-gloss. Slightly more rigid than gel but with a similar consistency. Holds stiff peaks and tool marks.

**Hard Molding Paste:** Has the hardest finish, dries opaque and matte. Use to create tough, durable finishes. It can be carved when dry.

**Coarse Molding Paste:** Has a sandy texture, retains tool marks and dries opaque to a crystalline appearance. Use for building surfaces or as a ground.

**Light Molding Paste:** Dramatically reduces the weight that traditional molding paste would add. Holds peaks, dries opaque, matte finish, excellent ground for watercolor techniques.

**Modeling Paste:** Dries opaque, holds peaks and tool marks, and can be sanded or carved.

**Flexible Modeling Paste:** Dries opaque and matte. Use on a flexible or rigid support. Holds peaks and tool marks and contains marble dust.

**Light Modeling Paste:** Lightweight, flexible, thick, and dries to a matte opaque white. Holds tool marks.

**Gloss Medium:** General purpose liquid for glazes, extending color, enhancing gloss, and increasing film integrity. Oil-like and resinous, promoting flow and leveling.

**Matte Medium:** General purpose, pourable, extends color, decreases gloss, and increases film integrity. It can be used to create a clear ground, instead of gesso.

**Fluid Matte Medium:** Use with fluid acrylics. Extends colors, decreases gloss, and increases film integrity.

**Silkscreen Medium:** Increases work time and retards paint from drying on the screen.

**Glazing Medium:** Slow drying and improves "brushability". Use for wet-in-wet techniques, glazing, and faux finishing techniques.

**Gesso:** Used as a ground to improve adherence of colors. Not a medium and not intended to be mixed with paints. Keep this one as a primer!

**Retarder:** Used to slow drying time, for wet-in-wet techniques, and helps to reduce skinning on your paint palette. Must be used as an additive to your paint as it contains no binding agent.

**Wetting Agent or Flow Release:** Add this to your water to improve the absorption of color into porous surfaces. It causes rich staining on watercolor paper.

**Fabric Medium:** You can find fabric mediums in several brands.

- **Liquitex:** Enhances workability, color blending, and flow for fabric painting as it controls color bleeding and reduces stiffness. This medium can be used as a flow medium for other techniques.
- **Decoart:** This product can be found in the craft painting section of your local hobby shop. It improves penetration and bonding with fabric fibers and is permanent and washable.
- **Golden GAC 900:** Mix with acrylic colors to produce a paint that offers a soft finish with laundering stability, excellent for clothing artists. Must be heat-set, use with adequate ventilation when setting as it releases low levels of formaldehyde.

**Glass & Tile Medium:** This medium allows for painting on slick surfaces and increases the durability of the paint. It provides a tooth for the paint to cling onto. It can be found wherever they sell Folkart craft paints or local craft and hobby shops.

I would like to mention that acrylic paint will stick to glass by itself, but it is not permanent. Using this medium increases the paint's surface durability and longevity. If you desire to paint a lot of glassware or want a permanent solution, I suggest you investigate other options.

I would recommend Pebeo glass paint as it bears qualities you won't find in other glass paints. It is a thermo-hardening paint which makes it permanent and non-toxic. Although the hardening process requires excellent ventilation, so find a used oven for your garage and bake during warmer months!

There are many more mediums that you will find in your local craft stores specifically designed to be used with craft-grade paints which I won't list here. This list provides you with a wide range of information for most applications and should be sufficiently overwhelming for even the most advanced painters!

# TERMINOLOGY: COLORS & PAINT

**Hue:** The name of a color. More specifically it is the precise identification of a position of a color in the hue position band. Some colors may lean toward their neighbor while others are on center. Also, if a paint color says hue at the end of it, it is a replacement for mineral colors that may be unavailable, too expensive, toxic, or considered fugitive colors. They will generally yield higher intensities than the colors they imitate.

**Chroma**: Also known as saturation or intensity. It describes how brilliant or subdued the color looks. The Chroma of color decreases with distance when painting landscapes for example. The brightness or intensity of a color can be identified by a number range of 0 to 20. Natural grey has no trace of chroma and is rated 0. The brighter the color the higher the number. This information can be found on the paint label.

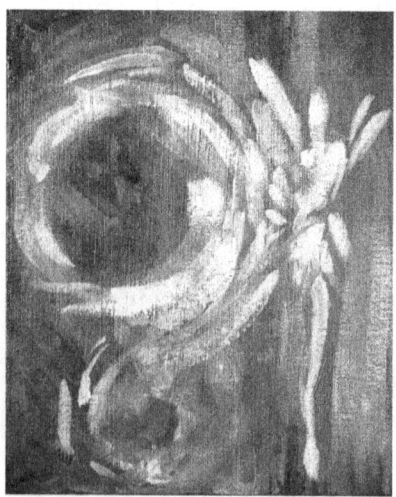

**Primary Color:** There are three primary colors; red, yellow & blue, which can be used to create secondary & tertiary colors. No other colors can be mixed to create primary colors. They are primary to any paint palette, and it is often suggested that you keep a warm and cool color set and mix all other colors you desire.

**Secondary Colors:** A color created by mixing two primary colors. Orange, Violet, and Green.

**Tertiary Colors:** A color created by mixing a primary color with a secondary color. Yellow Green, Blue Green, Blue Violet, Red Violet, Red Orange, and Yellow Orange.

**Primary Color Wheel:** A color circle that organizes colors and shows the relationships between primary, secondary, and tertiary colors.

**Additional Color Wheels:** In addition to the primary color wheel there is RGB, CMYK, and pigment primary color wheel sometimes referred to as a mixing color wheel. Understanding the differences will help you understand color more fully.

- **RGB:** This is an additive color wheel used for television or computer screens. Additive color refers to how we view color in light. RGB stands for red, green, and blue. When you add all these colors of light together you have white. (helpful to those who like to play with digital images)
- **CMYK:** This is a color wheel used in printing and stands for cyan (in the blue family), magenta (in the red family), yellow, and black (which is what you get when you add them all together.
- **Pigment Primary Color Wheel or Mixing Color Wheel:** It's good to know the CMYK colors to better understand a painter's palette could replace the use of primary blue with the use of cyan and replace primary red with magenta to create a wider range of color mixes producing better greens and violets than the typical primary color wheel.

**Color Temperature:** This refers to the level of warmth within any certain color. It also describes the warmth or coolness of a light source. "Warm white" generally means a yellowish type of white, and "cool white" means a blueish white.

**Warm Colors:** Colors that fall to the left of the color wheel are considered warm colors. Primary Red is the dominant warm color. To help you remember this, think of red as fire which is warm. Paintings that incorporate more reds and oranges are considered warm paintings. Yellow is generally considered to be a warm color. However, some contain small amounts of blue making them a greenish yellow, and therefore may appear much cooler.

**Cool Colors:** Colors that fall to the right of the color wheel. Primary blue is the dominant cool color. Remember this as you think of the cooling effects of water. Paintings that contain more blues and greens are considered cool paintings.

**Muddy Colors:** Refers to colors that have become so neutralized between warm and cool they look like mud. To correct this problem simply add more cool color *or* more warm color to the mixture to push the color up and out of the muddiness.

**Intensity:** The brightness or strength of a hue. To change the intensity of a color, add various degrees of white, black, or its complementary color. See Chroma.

**Complementary Colors:** Colors that fall directly opposite each other on the color wheel. Like red and green, or blue and orange. When compliments are mixed in various degrees, they create shades, and the intensity of either color is muted or neutralized. This method for creating paint shades can produce more vibrant shades than adding black. Placing compliments next to each other makes both colors appear more intense and vivid.

**Split Complementary Colors:** This is a set of three colors, your initial color, and the two colors immediately to the right and left of its complement. An example would be Yellow, Red Violet, and Blue Violet. The violets will enhance the yellow but not with the same degree of intensity as the direct complement of Purple. Mixing this selection of colors will yield a well-balanced grey.

**Triad Colors:** Those colors that fall at the points of a triangle when it is placed inside of the color wheel. The three primary colors form a triad. Red, Blue, and Yellow for example.

**Tetradic:** Rectangle color scheme, uses four equally spaced colors on the color wheel. Two complementary pairs. This combination offers plenty of possibilities and works best if one color becomes dominant.

**Analogous Colors:** Three Colors that lay next to each other on the color wheel. Such as Red, Red Orange, and Orange for example.

**Value:** The lightness or darkness of a hue, compared to white and black. There are 10 value steps ranging from pure black at level 0 to pure white at level 10. The higher the number the lighter the color. You may find the value of a color on some paint labels. Value or contrast is the first thing your eye sees when observing a work of art. Dark against light draws the eye.

**Saturation:** Also known as Chroma or Intensity. It describes how brilliant or subdued the color looks.

**Tint:** You tint a hue by adding white. To keep tints from appearing "chalky", add a touch of the color residing above your tinted color on the color wheel to sharpen or freshen it up.

**Shade:** You shade a hue by adding black. To keep a shade from appearing "muddy" add a touch of the color that resides below your shaded color on the color wheel. Shades can also be produced by adding the complement to a color, at various degrees.

**Tone:** A color that has been lightened or darkened by adding gray.

**Pigments:** A dry substance added to the paint mixture giving the paint its color. The type of pigment determines the opacity of the color. The pigment is classified into two categories based on chemical composition - Organic pigments and Inorganic pigments.

**Modern Pigments:** Also referred to as Organic Pigments. These are translucent or transparent high chroma with high tinting strength such as Quinacridone Magenta, Hansa Yellow Medium, Phthalo Blue (Green Shade), Phthalo Green (Blue Shade), and Naphthol Red Light. They are formed from complex carbon chemistry and are synthetic pigments.

**Mineral Pigments:** These pigments are derived from natural minerals and ores. They are moderate to high opacity, with low chroma and low tinting strength such as Cadmiums, Titanium White, Zinc White, and Yellow Ochre. However, Zinc is an exception to this rule, this white is transparent.

**Permanency:** Refers to the lightfastness of a color when exposed to ultraviolet light. There are three categories, Lightfastness I will exhibit no color change after 100 years of indoor light exposure, good for outdoor murals. Lightfastness II is suited for all indoor applications but not exterior painting. Lightfastness III is considered a fugitive color and is not recommended for permanent works.

**Opaque:** An opaque color is neither transparent nor translucent. An opaque color has good coverage, or hiding power, and does not allow colors underneath to show through. This is due to the light not passing through it.

**Translucent:** Not entirely opaque or transparent. Some light travels through this layer revealing some of the color below.

**Transparent:** Allows light to pass through so that colors underneath can be seen. It has the least covering power.

**Masstone:** The undiluted color of a pigment. When a color is applied thickly covering the surface and no other color from below it shows through it. Some colors have a similar masstone and undertone.

**Undertone:** You will see the undertone of a paint color when you spread it thinly over a white surface. An undertone will appear as a lighter value of the masstone. With Quinacridones or Phthalo colors, the undertone can be quite different from the masstone. With these colors, you will experience shifts in the hue.

**Tinting Strength:** The ability of a color to change the character of another color. You may discover any color's tinting strength by adding it to Titanium White. Weaker tinting colors create pastel mixtures while stronger colors create darker mixtures.

**Viscosity:** Refers to the fluidity of the paint. High viscosity is a paint that resists movement, like heavy body paint. Low viscosity is more fluid like craft paint.

**Impasto:** Thickly applied paint.

**Mediums:** These are added to paints to change certain qualities of the paint. They generally contain no pigment.

**Additives:** These contain no binder and require correct usage for the best results. They are not meant to be used alone and must be mixed with paint colors. They include Retarder, Flow Release, and Thinner.

**Isolation Coat:** a clear, non-removable coating that serves to separate the paint surface from the varnish. It protects the painting if or when the varnish is removed and seals any absorbent areas creating an even surface for varnish to be applied to.

**High Key:** refers to light value colors, mid-tone to white.

**Low Key:** It refers to dark value colors, mid-tone to black.

**EXPERIMENTAL EXERCISE:**

**Create your own color wheel using only the colors you currently have. Beginning with yellow in the noon position. Continue around the wheel using the chart below.**

**If you do not have any paint, purchase a**

**red, yellow, and blue to create the following.**

*Yellow Green @ 1:00 pm*
*Green @ 2:00 pm*
*Blue @ 4:00 pm*
*Blue Violet @ 5:00 pm*
*Purple @ 6:00 pm*
*Red Violet @ 7:00 pm*
*Red @ 8:00 pm*
*Red Orange @ 9:00 pm*
*Orange @ 10:00 pm*
*Yellow Orange @ 11:00 pm*

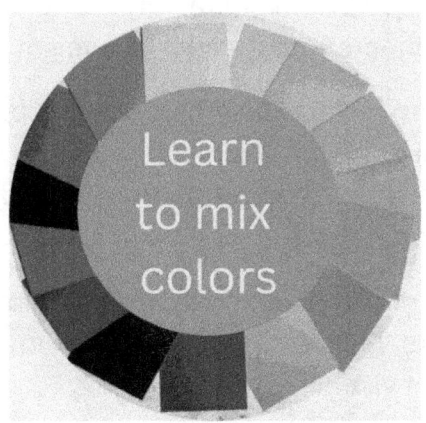

43

# TERMINOLOGY: COMPOSITION

**Composition:** The arrangement of subject matter or elements within your painting that will create eye flow and visual balance.

**Positive Space:** The figure or object that is being painted.

**Negative Space:** The environment, air, or "space" around the figure or object being painted.

**Rule of Thirds:** The idea that the most interesting compositions are where the primary element is off-center. Divide the paint area into thirds vertically and horizontally, then place the primary element where lines cross, creating a focal point. Each area can have interest, one is dominant. Use the lines themselves as a guide for the alignment of larger elements.

**Visual Center:** Slightly above and to the right of the actual mathematical center, the natural placement of visual focus.

**Balance:** Visual equilibrium or stability made by the arrangement of objects with their visual weight.

**Symmetry or Formal Balance:** The organization of elements along a horizontal or vertical axis, normally identical elements on both sides of the axis with weight distributed evenly like a mirrored image.

**Approximate Symmetry:** As above but with similar, not identical elements. Elements may give a feeling of exactness but vary to prevent visual monotony.

**Asymmetry or Informal Balance:** Elements on either side of the axis are not identical, they may vary in size, color, and shape but are organized to create a feeling of equilibrium and balance.

**Radial Symmetry:** Two or more identical forces distributed around a center point, or rotating forces which create visual circular movement, similar or identical elements radiating from a point.

**Proximity:** When you have many elements that are near one another, the brain tends to group them so that they become one visual unit.

**Repetition:** Adds visual interest, helps identify elements that belong together, adds consistency, and creates visual unity. The repetition of color, spatial relationships, shape, and texture can all create unity.

**Unity:** A combination of elements working together to create harmony. It is the relationship between individual parts and the whole of the composition.

**Contrast:** Adding interest through light/dark, warm/cool, large/small, and is most effective when high or strong. Contrast can be used to direct focus but can lead to visual confusion if not strong enough.

**Dynamics:** The arrangement of elements to create the illusion of movement which can add a characteristic of restful/calm or active/energetic. There are four basic forms.

    1.) **Rhythmic:** This creates order and predictability. A regular rhythm is created when the space between, or the elements themselves, are similar in size or length.

2.) **Arrhythmic:** An unstructured rhythm that adds visual interest. A flowing rhythm gives a sense of movement and is organic by nature.

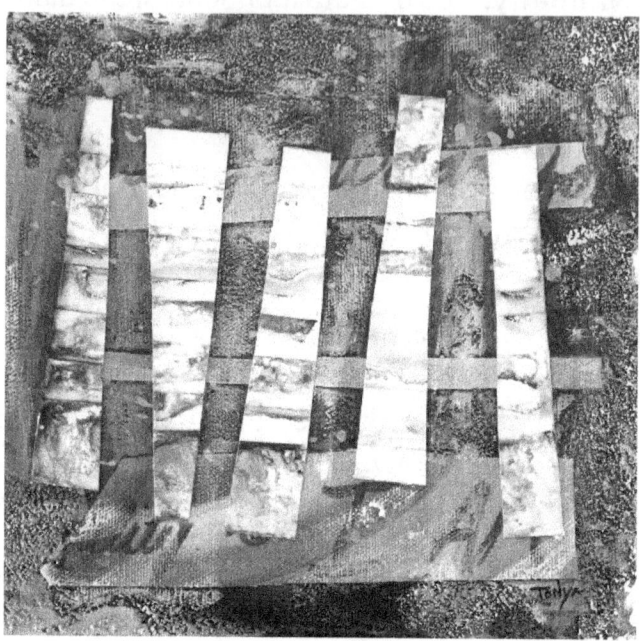

3.) **Random Rhythm:** Has no defined order and creates spontaneity.
4.) **Directional Rhythm:** Elements are placed in a way that leads the eyes in a specific direction. A progressive rhythm is a sequence of forms through progressive steps.

**Emphasis:** A focal point, or center of interest, is the area that visually dominates, or is eye-catching. This can be achieved in repetition by creating a break in the basic structure or pattern, which will cause your eye to pause. It can be achieved by contrast or accentuating an area to separate it from another. It can also be achieved using color, texture, scale, or shape.

**Proportion:** Comparison of dimensions, or comparison of the distribution of elements. It is the relationship of scale between elements or the relationship between an object and its parts.

**Dominance:** Dominance can be established with color, shape, or size. It suggests that certain elements should assume more importance than others and will often resolve where the eye goes first. There are three stages of dominance.

1.) **Dominant:** The object with the most visual weight has a primary emphasis and advances to the foreground.
2.) **Sub Dominant:** The object with secondary emphasis and stands in the middle ground.
3.) **Subordinate:** That which recedes to the background and has the least visual weight.

**Closure:** The brain tends to fill in missing information when it perceives an object as having missing pieces.

**Continuance:** Once your eye begins to move in a direction, it will continue until something more significant catches its attention.

**Similarity:** Items of similar size, shape, and/or color tend to be grouped together by the brain.

**Three Spot Composition:** This is created when three points of interest are used, with one of them being the dominant, or center of interest.

**Steelyard Composition:** A large mass that is counterbalanced by a smaller mass, with the center of interest being closer to the larger mass or the larger mass itself.

**"L" Composition:** This is a variation of the Steelyard composition. Created when either the negative or the positive space is arranged in such a manner that an "L" shape has been formed along the edges of the image.

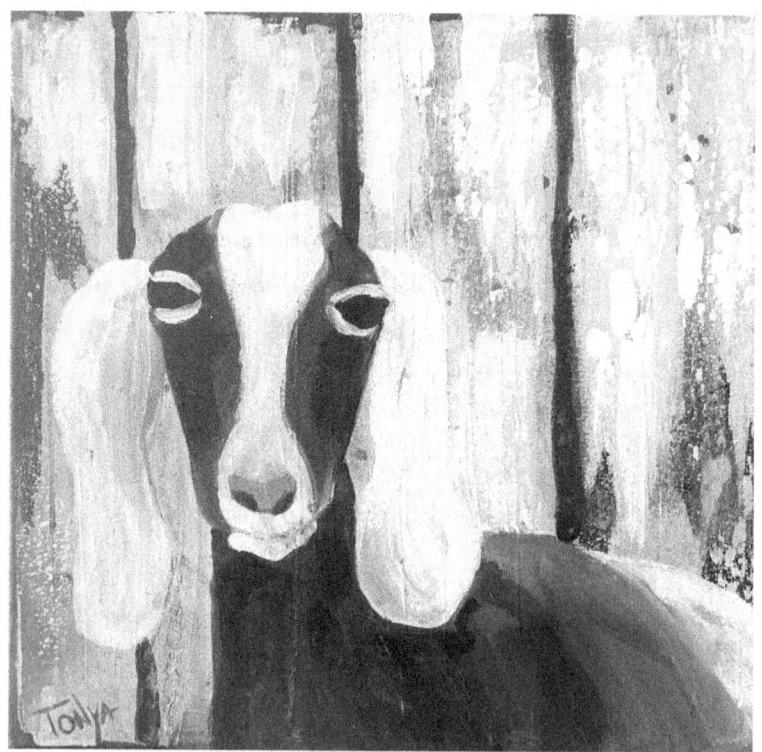

## A BIT ABOUT COLOR

Without light, we cannot see colors. When natural light hits any surface, its energy is absorbed, bent, or reflected. Black absorbs almost all light energy, while white reflects the energy. Colored surfaces will absorb some of the light waves and reflect others. This is how we see color.

Paint colors come in two types, mineral colors, and modern colors. Mineral colors are derived from natural minerals or ores, while modern colors are synthetically manufactured from complex carbon chemistry.

Paint labels give a good degree of information beyond the color name you may want to take note of, such as the permanence of a color. This information can reveal if a color is good for outdoor mural work or is considered a fugitive color. Look at the label to discover if the lightfastness is I, II, or III. In this case, I is high permanence.

The label will also reveal the value of a color, on a scale of 0 to 10, the higher the number the lighter the value. The chroma of a color will be on a scale of 0 to 20 with the number increasing with brightness. A neutral grey, for instance, will be a 0 as it has no chroma. You can also find if a color is opaque, translucent, or transparent and what its viscosity may be.

Color wheels are not all created equal. For example, light source colors such as your television and computer screens use an RGB color wheel. This wheel utilizes the colors Red Green and Blue as primaries to produce color mixes.

Printing colors, or CMYK are used for printing brochures and business cards for example. They include Cyan, Magenta, and Yellow as primary and black for creating shades. These four colors produce all the colors you see in printed materials.

Basic color wheels use Red Yellow Blue as primary colors to give a basic understanding of color mixing. Red mixed with yellow makes orange, Blue mixed with red makes purple, and Yellow mixed with Blue makes green. This is key to understanding colors, but it is not the complete story.

With so many colors available to choose from, how do we know where to start?

Golden artist colors provide a color mixing chart on their website to help you understand how to utilize 8 basic colors in combination with one another to create a vast array of interesting color mixing solutions. These colors are as follows; Hansa Yellow Light and Medium, Naphthol Red Light, Quinacridone Magenta, Anthraquinone Blue, Phthalo Blue (Green Shade=GS), Phthalo Green (Blue Shade=BS), and White. Learn more about these colors in the list below.

Many artists prefer what is called a pigment primary color wheel which places the anchors as Cyan rather than "blue", Quinacridone Magenta rather than "red", and Primary Yellow as it is a neutral yellow. Meaning it has no bias or does not lean toward orange (Cadmium Yellow) or green (Lemon Yellow).

If you are painting traditional landscapes or portraits, keep in mind that a palette that contains the Cadmium colors will give you a more natural look. Cadmiums are mineral colors. You may find colors that will be titled Cadmium Red Hue. This is a chemical replication of a true mineral color. These colors may be produced because they are a lower-cost alternative, the mineral may produce a fugitive color, or because the mineral pigment cannot be suspended in the acrylic polymer emulsion due to its particle size.

A basic three-color palette might include Quinacridone Crimson, Azo Yellow Medium, and Phthalo Blue. Or try Permanent Rose in place of Crimson. These colors are considered good primary choices. You will be able to create a nice selection of mixes with this color palette, add white for tints, and if you prefer, black for shades. Many artists prefer to use a mix of their primary colors to create a black and may use this combination to create shades.

Look for single pigment colors for the purest of colors or "unmixed" colors and use Neutral Grey 5 to adjust value and chroma without altering hue.

A mineral color palette might include Cadmium Red, Cadmium Yellow, Yellow Ochre, Cobalt Blue, and Ultramarine Blue. These colors are good for natural-looking landscapes as they more closely replicate the tones of the natural world. They are opaque inorganic pigments that limit your color mixing possibilities and can become muddy. Solve this issue by adding a small amount of modern color to restore any lost chroma. It is important to note that the qualities of modern colors sometimes show up in a mineral color.

With the introduction of modern colors, you will have a more extensive range than with the traditional mineral pigments. These colors may, however, be more transparent. Use Titanium White to make an opaquer color mixture, or Zinc White to maintain transparency. You can also keep Yellow Ochre on hand as this is also an opaque mixing option.

Consider the following modern colors for a broader range of mixing potential.

**Hansa Yellow Light:** resembles Cadmium Yellow Light and makes more intense tints and cleaner secondary colors. This color has a green bias, producing wonderful lime and light green colors. Golden's new color Benzimidazolone Yellow is comparable to Hansa Yellow and comes in a light and medium.

**Hansa Yellow Medium:** is sometimes considered the perfect yellow. Its masstone is like Cadmium Yellow but it is more transparent and offers more control when mixing. It's a high-tinting organic pigment good for glazing and like Hansa Yellow Light makes cleaner secondary colors. This color has an orange bias which creates a beautiful range of oranges.

**Naphthol Red Light:** is a strong bright warm red that leans to the red-orange part of the color spectrum, making it perfect for mixing oranges. It is a deep, intense, permanent, semi-transparent color that is a good replacement for Cadmium Red, giving cleaner mixes. Will create a nice rose or pink tint.

**Quinacridone Magenta:** is a superb mixing red and makes high-key tints. A single pigment color for brilliant reds and pinks as well as beautiful transparent violets as it has a purple bias.

**Anthraquinone Blue:** is a red-leaning primary blue ideal for unusual color mixes. It has a very dark value, optical black when unmixed, the closest single pigment to mimic Indigo. It is transparent with a strong tinting strength. You may find it listed as Delft Blue, Indian Blue, and Faience Blue.

**Phthalo Blue (green shade) :** is a bright brilliant blue with extremely high tinting strength. A cool blue with a bias towards green can be used for glazing techniques. Keep in mind that this color can easily overpower other colors in the mixing process. It is a transparent staining color that produces beautiful skies in landscape painting. Excellent for mixing paynes grey and a lovely blue range including turquoise.

**Phthalo Green (blue shade) :** produces a wide range of color mixtures, from transparent subtle natural colors to strong brilliant opaque colors. It is a transparent staining color with extremely high tinting strength. This color may look unrealistic if used alone but is an excellent choice for mixing.

**With the above palette:** you will find a variety of ways to create rich blacks and a wide range of greys. Add white to your collection and try out this color palette as an alternative to traditional mineral colors and you'll create brighter, cleaner-looking color mixes in a much wider range.

These are all just suggestions for creating your first palette of color. Mix and match as you wish, as you try these different colors, you will find your favorites.

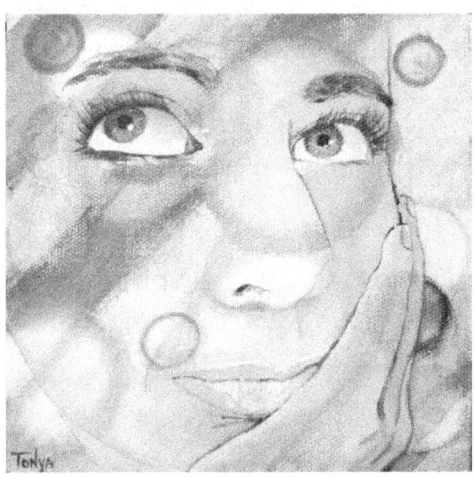

The following will help you in choosing whites, blacks, and greys, and offers a bit of information regarding color mixtures.

**Naphthol Red Light:** which leans toward orange, helps to balance the Quinacridone Magenta which leans more toward violet producing a more neutral red.

**Quinacridone Magenta:** with Hansa Yellow Medium reveals a wider selection of intense reds and oranges. Mixtures with Phthalo Blue (Green Shade=GS) allow deep reds and maroons.

**Equal parts Phthalo Green (Blue Shade) and Phthalo Blue (Green Shade):** result in producing a beautiful turquoise. Phthalo mixtures with Hansa Yellow Medium produce a great range of greens, particularly subtle yellow greens. This green also helps create a diverse range of earth tones.

**Yellow Ochre:** a natural earth color that helps "warm" and subdue color mixtures. When mixed with Titanium White it lightens colors offering an opaque alternative to creating a pastel range. When combined with Zinc White, Yellow Ochre becomes transparent, making it suitable for creating glazing mixtures or adding deeper, warmer tones to brighter colors. I recommend using Yellow Ochre to achieve a different color palette.

**Zinc White:** is an extremely transparent white for subtle tinting and glazing.

**Titanium White:** this is the whitest white and most opaque. Great for creating more opaque mixtures, especially pastel tones, and it is a general-purpose color.

**Mixing White:** a more transparent white with reduced tinting strength, making it good for strong tints, glazing, and toning down colors.

**Iridescent White:** captures the effect of "light interference". Mixed with or painted over other colors to create pearlized effects.

*EXPERIMENTAL EXERCISE:*

*This experiment is to help you understand the differences between...*

- *Variations of White. Titanium vs. Zinc.*
- *Masstone & Undertone*
- *Opaque & Transparent color*

*Start by applying a thick opaque stroke of each white. Choose any color and do the same. This will show you the Masstone of each. Then scrape through each color to reveal its undertone.*

*Create a value scale of your chosen color by mixing it with Titanium white graduating from a very light tint to its original out-of-the-tube color.*

*Now create a value scale of your chosen color by mixing with Zinc white.*

**Ivory Black:** is a brown-black with moderate tinting strength and is a good general-purpose color.

**Lamp Black:** is a blueish black and opaque.

**Mars Black:** is a denser, more neutral black with stronger tinting power.

**Davy's Gray:** this is a terrific mixing grey, great for keeping a clean toning down of color, without the mudding effect caused by adding black.

**Graphite Grey:** is a dark grey that is not made of black and white. It too can be excellent for toning down colors.

**Payne's Gray:** is a very dark grey with a strong blue undertone. It produces a purer color mixer than when mixing with black.

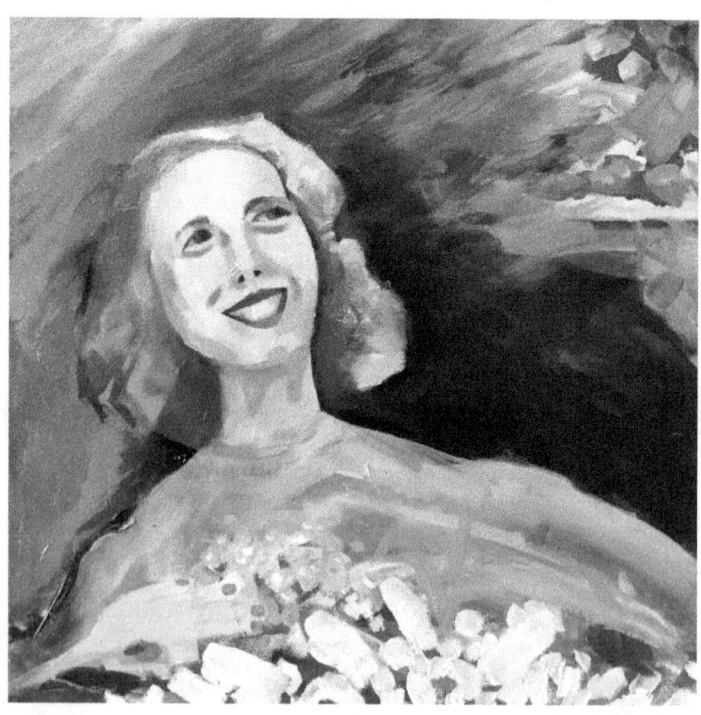

# COLOR MIXING RECIPES

**Orange:** Mix equal parts of **Red** and **Yellow**.

**Green:** Mix equal parts of **Blue** and **Yellow** or use **Cyan + Yellow**.

**Purple:** Mix equal parts of **Red** and **Blue**.

**Cyan + Magenta:** Becomes Primary Blue.

**Magenta + Yellow:** Becomes Primary Red.

**Cyan + Yellow + Magenta:** Becomes black.

**Teal:** Mix **Blue** with a small amount of **Green**.

**Turquoise:** Combine equal parts **Phthalo Blue GS** with **Phthalo Green BS**.

**Peach:** Combine **Red** and **Yellow**, then add **White** to lighten.

**Gray:** Mix equal parts of **Black** and **White**. For a warmer shade of gray, add a touch of **Burnt Umber** or **Ultramarine Blue**.

**Skin Tones:** Start with equal parts of **Red, Yellow**, and **White** to create a base skin tone. Adjust with small amounts of **Raw Umber** for darker tones or **White** for lighter tones. Or consider adding a touch of **Raw Sienna**.

**Brown:** Mix equal parts of **Red, Yellow**, and **Blue**. Alternatively, you can mix **Orange** and **Black** for a darker brown.

**Earthtones:** Combining medium shades of green with lime greens alongside orange-reds and orange yellows provides a wide range of earthy colors. By blending organic pigments, you can preserve vivid and clear colors.

### EXPERIMENTAL EXERCISE:

*This experiment is to help you learn to mix a wide range of earth colors.*

*Mix a generous amount of Hansa Yellow with a tiny bit of Phthalo Green BS. Remember that the mixing power of a Phthalo is extraordinarily rich. Do not underestimate its power! This mixture will create a bright green.*

*Next, mix a fair amount of Quinacridone Magenta with a small amount of Hansa Yellow. This mixture will create a bright red.*

*Paint a small square of each color mixture on a canvas board.*

*Then mix equal amounts of each of your primary mixtures and place a small square next to your previous squares on your canvas.*

*Now experiment with a fair amount of one primary mixture with a small amount of the other and vice versa. Make a square of each new mixture on your canvas board.*

*Consider making a range of mixes from one primary mixture to the other. Giving yourself insight into each small step in between and helping you form a long-lasting memory of your painting experiment.*

*I always suggest to my painting students that they use a fine-tip marker or pen to make notes on the canvas board next to each square they paint and utilize the back of the canvas board for more extensive notetaking.*

*Keep all your experimental canvas boards to create a book for yourself. Stack them together, drill two or three holes along the left-hand side, and use string or D-rings to bind them all together.*

*Keep this book in your workspace as a reference tool for future color mixing.*

**Painting Hair:**

When painting hair, remember that curved areas are shaded on the top and bottom with the highlight being placed in the middle. Some of the shaded areas will extend into the highlighted area.

Areas of long hair will generally be thicker at the head and thinner at the ends. Shorter hair can make a face look younger while longer hair can make a face look older.

As with many subjects start with a medium value as a basecoat, shading with a darker value, and highlighting with a litter value.

**Try these color mixtures for painting hair:**

- Naples Yellow + Raw Umber
- Yellow Ochre + Raw Umber
- Cadmium Yellow + Burnt Umber
- Raw Umber + Yellow Ochre + Burnt Sienna

**Painting Skin Tones:**

Use the following suggestions for natural-looking skin tones...

- Burnt Sienna + White
- Burnt Sienna + Raw Umber + White
- Burnt Sienna + Alizarin Crimson + White
- Burnt Sienna + Cadmium Yellow + White
- Raw Umber + White

Consider using **Alizarin Crimson** or **Cerulean Blue** to tilt a color slightly. These are not the only color recipes that will work. These are simply suggestions to get you off to a great start.

**Painting Lip Colors:**

Try these color mixtures for painting lips...

- Burnt Sienna + White with a touch of Alizarin Crimson
- Burnt Sienna + White with a touch of Cadmium Red
- Naples Yellow + Cadmium Red

Again, these are not the only color combinations that will work for you. You don't need to go out and purchase a **Naples Yellow** if you have something else. These are possible solutions, and you can mix what colors you already have to potentially accomplish a nice lip color. It's important to experiment with your colors to see what is possible.

**Painting Eyes:**

Try these color mixtures for painting eyes…

- Raw Umber + Prussian Blue
- Yellow Ochre + Ultramarine Blue
- Naples Yellow + Prussian Blue
- Prussian Blue + Raw Umber + White
- Raw Umber + Raw Sienna + White

**Summer Sky:**

- Ultramarine Blue + White

Add additional blue to your mixture as you move away from the horizon and consider adding a touch of darker blue closer to the top of the canvas. Something like a **Phthalo Blue GS** or **Prussian Blue.** Add **Cobalt Bue** or **Cerulean Blue** for a bit more drama.

**Clouds:**

Clouds can be anywhere from yellow and pink to grey and blue. Let's start with this conversation with big fluffy clouds.

- Titanium White + Ultramarine Blue + Raw Umber
- Titanium White + Ultramarine Blue + Burnt Sienna
- Titanium White + Raw Sienna + Rose Madder

- Titanium White + Prussian Blue + Raw Umber

Use this combination for a basic fluffy cloud by adding a small amount of **Ultramarine Blue** and a tiny bit of **Raw Umber** to your white. When painting the cloud start at the bottom and add more white to your mixture as you move toward the top.

Try a combination of Ultramarine Blue, Burnt Sienna, and small amounts of Titanium White to create value changes for the shadow areas of your cloud. The Blue color is dominant. Then use **Titanium White** with a small amount of **Ultramarine Blue** and a tiny amount of **Burnt Sienna**, using more burnt sienna in the mix for distant cloud highlights to make the clouds recede. Where white is dominant. When painting the sky for these clouds add **Cobalt Blue** to the mix.

Here are some other color options you may want to give a try when painting clouds.

Raw Sienna + Rose Madder + Ultramarine Blue (Darken with purple or add Cerulean to warm it up) Paint your sky with a combination of Cerulean, Ultramarine Blue, and Titanium White using more Cerulean as you move closer to the horizon.

As a bonus, I will mention here that clouds are smaller and closer to one another as they approach the horizon. Larger with more "space" around them as you move toward the top of your canvas. This will help you create depth in your landscape paintings.

**Tropical Ocean Water:**

Create a variety of mixes using the following colors.

- **Phthalo Blue GS + Cadmium Yellow + Titanium White** adding more yellow as you move into the foreground. This will give the appearance of shallow water.
- **Ultramarine Blue + Titanium White.** Use this mixture to add the reflection of the sky into the water.
- Use a combination of these colors to create a refraction of light.

**Wet Sand:**

Sand can look different in different parts of the world, so you'll need to decide if it's white or some shade of tan and remember that sand is darker when wet. Combine a small amount of a warm yellow like **Cadmium Yellow** with a touch of purple like **Dioxazine Purple** with a considerable amount of **Titanium White**. White sand requires more white paint in your mixture.

- Try these additional color combinations for variants in your sand.
- Titanium White + Hansa Yellow Medium + Dioxazine Purple
- Titanium White + Yellow Ochre + Ultramarine Blue
- Titanium White + Try a Sienna or Raw Sienna in combination with any violet or blue-violet in a tiny amount.

When painting abstractly or expressionistically it's quite possible you could choose to throw all these recipes out the door and paint skin-tone pink, blue, or green. Maybe all three if you like. The sky is the limit, which could be painted yellow if you like!

You are the creator. Let your imagination move you. Feel your way through a painting and think of yourself as a scientist who is exploring color experimentation.

In other words, play and have fun!

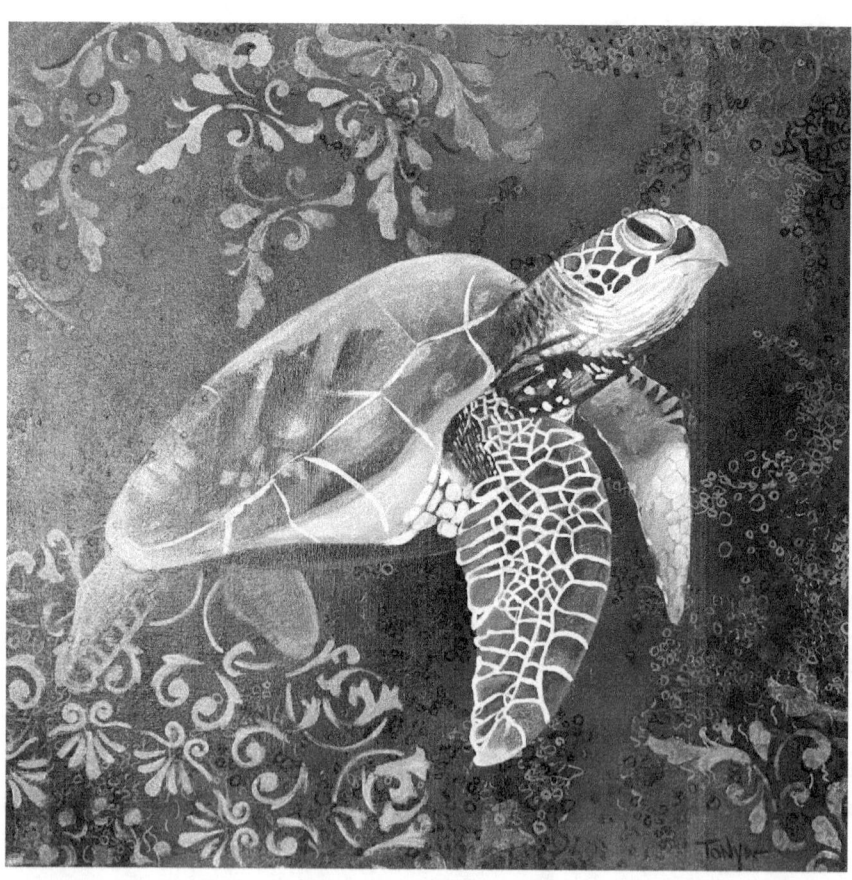

# ADDITIONAL HELPFUL HINTS

**Perspective:**

When painting landscapes, seascapes, and cityscapes, keep in mind that scale, contrast, details, chroma, and color temperature all decrease with distance. Objects will also become softer in their edges, so reduce any hard edges by softening distant items.

Overlapping objects help to describe what is in front or behind. Overlap shapes often to make spatial relationships clearer.

Blues, greens, and blue violets are cool colors that aid in the illusion of distance, as they are what we call receding colors. Compared to red, these colors will visually recede while red advances. Reds and oranges are warm advancing colors. Your violets and yellows, therefore, need to be leaning towards red to advance and a blue hue to recede.

Yellow is the most visible color. Specifically, fluorescent yellow, which looks like a yellow-green. It can overwhelm a painting, use it as pure color with caution, and subdue it when needed.

**One Point Perspective:**

One-point perspective begins with the Horizon Line. This line is always in front of you at eye level. If you look straight ahead without tipping your head up or down, the horizon line is formed where the sky meets the land. Whether sitting, standing, or crouching down, the horizon line moves with you.

The viewpoint is always located on the horizon line in the center of your field of vision. The vanishing point is always located on the horizon line. It is the place where all receding lines appear to converge.

**All images are made up of these two things:**

**Visual Approach:** A visual approach will help you see things in a new way and show you a way to expand your creativity. There are eight visual approaches.
Line, color, equalization, and dark-light pattern are considered abstract. While silhouette, form, local tone, and shadow are created by light. These subjects will be covered in my next workbook.

**Pattern of light and Dark:** (do not confuse with dark light pattern) A pattern of light and dark exists if there is an image. In other words, a degree of light and dark or any change in value must be present to create an image.

**Texture:** When a texture is big enough it can become a pattern, and a pattern can become texture with a difference in value.

**Edges:** Edges can be hard or soft. Hard edges draw the eye more than soft edges. Lost and found edges are sharp in some places and soft in others. The viewer's eye will connect broken lines.

**Positive & Negative shapes:** if you are painting a chair, the chair is considered the positive shape or space, and everything that is not the chair is the negative space.

Overlapping shapes help to define 3D space on a 2D picture plain (or canvas).

**Best Painting Advice:**

Rules are fantastic to know and sometimes need to be followed when it comes to painting images. Without a teacher, it's a long road to learn them. It's helpful to learn from someone who has been painting for some time. They can speed up your learning curve tremendously. Once you know the rules you will better understand how to break them.

I want to invite you to study with me. I've been painting, dare I say, for over 40 years. I've learned a lot in those years, and I want to share what I have learned with you before I leave this planet. If you would like that too, join me on Patreon at the "Artsy Spirit" level. **Patreon.com/CreativeSpiritStudios**

---

*"Go and make interesting mistakes, make amazing mistakes, make glorious and fantastic mistakes. Break rules. Leave the world more interesting for your being here. Make. Good. Art." – Neil Gaiman*

---

# ONE LAST MESSAGE

Your personality, your interests, and your personal desires help determine the outcome of your artmaking. We are each unique and should not compare ourselves to others. Learn to witness your growth and feel proud of your progress.

If I had not been second-guessing myself so much the journey would have been more enjoyable. If I had someone in my corner pointing the way, that would have helped too. That's why I would like to be here for you. I would like to help you navigate the journey by helping you avoid the potholes, find the bridges, and help you stay out of the gullies.

I'd like to be the one that helps you navigate your way to success. Whatever that means to you. Success is a relative word, and my success doesn't look like I thought it would. Yours probably won't either and that's okay!

*"Success is a relative word"*

If you've enjoyed this content and have received benefits from it, I'd like to invite you to follow me on my Patreon page for more great information. You have the flexibility to join at whatever level you currently find yourself, but if this is the kind of insights and knowledge that you'd like to have regularly please consider the "Artsy Spirit" level for helpful how-to videos & "Open Studio" nights.
**Patreon.com/CreativeSpiritStudios**

# ACKNOWLEDGMENTS

Through the years, many have shared ideas, mentoring, and support that have impacted my life, each in a different way. It's impossible to mention everyone as there have been so many. Please know that I appreciate you all tremendously.

To my family and friends, for having a greater belief in me sometimes than I could hold for myself.

To my partner who encourages my journey and distracts me with laughter when I get too serious.

To my business coaches who believed in my ability to grow beyond my imagination.

To my teachers who left breadcrumbs for me to follow, making the path that much easier to follow.

To my clients and students who became friends and colleagues, encouraging me to this day to keep creating art.

To all those who came and went from my life, leaving dents and damage. I wouldn't be who I am today without you. This is the good work you led me to do. Helping others live as large as their dreams no matter who or what stands in their way.

# ABOUT THE AUTHOR

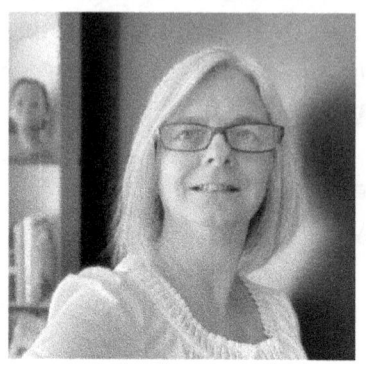

Tonya Henderson is a talented artist with a deep passion for helping others uncover their potential and grow both personally and creatively. As the owner of Creative Spirit Studios in the heart of Mid-Michigan, she has created a welcoming space where art flourishes and individuals can explore their creativity.

With a degree in Visual Communications from the Colorado Institute of Art in Denver and a diploma in Computer Graphics from the Dubner Training School in Hackensack, New Jersey, Tonya brings a wealth of knowledge and experience to her artistic practice. She has worked at WJRT-TV12, graphic design firms, and marketing agencies in Michigan & Colorado, honing her skills in graphic design for various media and marketing projects.

Tonya's artistic journey began with paintings inspired by spiritual concepts, where she intertwined biblical teachings with her explorations of metaphysics and the mysteries of the universe. This blend of influences set her on a profound new path, one that continues to shape her work today.

As a visionary artist, Tonya creates captivating spiritual paintings that capture the flow of energy, visionary landscapes, and vivid dreams. Her artwork invites viewers to glimpse unseen realms, alternate realities, and energetic pseudo-universes, reflecting her deep connection to nature, spirituality, and the interwoven fabric of all life. You can find her stunning pieces showcased at the Creative Spirit Studios Gallery, Holistic Expos, local shops, and various galleries.

In addition to her artwork, Tonya is a dedicated teacher of acrylic painting at the Flint Institute of Arts Museum School. She also offers drawing, painting, and art classes at her studio and various locations throughout Michigan. Beyond the classroom, she provides online training through her Patreon page, where she shares insights on artmaking, marketing, and personal growth, helping others navigate mindset challenges.

In her studio, Tonya's enthusiasm is infectious. She truly cares about her students, whether they are budding painters or seasoned art entrepreneurs, and is committed to ensuring they leave each session with a strong sense of accomplishment. As a coach, she takes her role seriously, all while making sure the creative journey is enjoyable and fulfilling. Tonya finds immense pride in guiding others as they manifest their dreams, considering it a true honor to work alongside artists as they develop their skills and nurture their art businesses.

For online assistance learn more about her teaching & coaching at **Patreon.com/CreativeSpiritStudios.**

**Don't forget to take advantage of these two special bonus resources created just for you!**

## Special <u>FREE</u> Bonus Gift for You

To help you to achieve more success faster, there are **FREE BONUS RESOURCES**:
- "Five Essential Resources I Use in My Art Business"
- "The Ultimate Guide to Starting a Fine Art Painting Business"

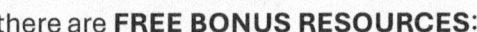

## ADDITIONAL RESOURCES

**Tonya Henderson is the Author of the following books:**

- Animal Portraits A to Z, found on Amazon.
- Angels Etc. - Patterns for Crafting, Coloring, and Embroidery, found at TonyaHenderson.com
- A Quick Reference Guide to Acrylic Painting, found at TonyaHenderson.com or on Amazon.
- 99 Ways to Make a Living as a Full-Time Artist, found on Amazon or TonyaHenderson.com.

**And soon to be released on Amazon:**

- Color Symbolism
- A New Adult Coloring Book

**Shop Original Art, Art Prints, and Digital Downloads...**

**Visit Tonya's website at:**
TonyaHenderson.com

**Or her Etsy Store at:**
PaintingPoet.Etsy.com

**Learn more about painting, marketing, and selling your art by joining Tonya on Patreon at the

**Artsy Spirit or Passionate Spirit levels and gain access to the Pricing, Selling, & Marketing Tips Workshop:**

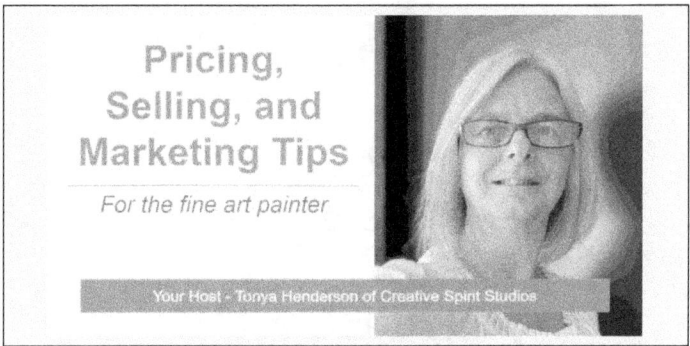

**Patreon.com/CreativeSpiritStudios**

**Here you'll find the following:**

- o Pricing, Selling, & Marketing Video Course.
- o Copyright Free Image Library for Reference & Inspiration.
- o Painting Instruction and Tips.
- o Mindset, Insights, and Tips.
- o Weekly Coaching Sessions.
- o Downloadable Business Documents.
- o Access to the Creative Spirit Studios community.

All content is accessible at the Passionate Spirit level. A great bundle of videos, documents, lessons, and coaching for one low monthly investment. With the opportunity to grow and learn in a community of artrepreneurs that will encourage & support you.

**Don't Forget to Get your Free Resource Guides here:**
https://mailchi.mp/3467c338d52e/join

# Special FREE Bonus Gift for You

To help you to achieve more success faster, there are

## FREE BONUS RESOURCES

for you at:

https://mailchi.mp/3467c338d52e/join

**DISCOVER MORE ABOUT THE AUTHOR AT THE FOLLOWING WEBSITES:**

www.TonyaHenderson.com

www.Patreon.com/CreativeSpiritStudios